THE HAND THAT HOLDS ME

Michael Rogness

AUGSBURG Publishing House • Minneapolis

THE HAND THAT HOLDS ME

Scripture quotations unless otherwise noted are from the Revised Standard Version of the Bible, copyright 1946, 1952, and 1971 by the Division of Christian Education of the National Council of Churches.

Quotations from the play "Peer Gynt" on pp. 43-46 are from the 1954 edition published by Caxton House.

Quotations from the song "Dulcinea" on pp. 106-107 are 1965 © Copyright, Andrew Scott, Inc., Helena Music Corp., Music by Mitch Leigh, Words by Joe Darion. Used by permission.

Library of Congress Cataloging in Publication Data

Rogness, Michael.
   THE HAND THAT HOLDS ME.

   1. Grace (Theology) 2. Good works (Theology)
3. Justification. 4. Christian life—Lutheran authors.
I. Title
BT761.2.R595   1984   234   84-14449
ISBN 0-8066-2093-5

Manufactured in the U.S.A.   APH 10-2943

  2   3   4   5   6   7   8   9   0   1   2   3   4   5   6   7   8   9

*To my mother and father,
from whom I learned firsthand
what grace is.*

Contents

1

A Free Lunch

A dissatisfied man wanted to find life's true meaning. First he asked his pastor. Next he went to church headquarters. Then he went to a theological seminary. He listened to everything that learned men and women could tell him about the meaning of life.

Still wanting to learn more, he traveled to the Vatican and was able to speak with the pope. Then he went to Geneva and spoke with the staff members of the World Council of Churches. All the while as he journeyed he asked people for the meaning of life. Finally he heard of a holy man—supposedly the holiest man in all Asia— who sat high in the Himalayas, isolated from the world, contemplating and meditating on life all his waking hours.

Our searcher flew to New Delhi, traveled by bus to a village below the mountains, and then set out on a long trek far above the timberline to the barren cave, where he found the aged sage sitting.

He sat down beside the man and asked, "Great sir, long have I searched for the meaning of life, and my quest has brought me from across the world to learn your wisdom. Tell me, what is the true meaning of life?"

The old man's eyes glanced at the traveler, then gazed into the heavens with a faraway look. He sat still for a long time, barely breathing. Finally he turned back, leaned forward, took a deep breath, and said in a quiet voice: "The meaning of life? The meaning life, young man, is this . . . ." (The traveler leaned forward in eager anticipation.) *"There is no such thing as a free lunch!"*

There is some truth in that silly story, and that truth is this: According to the wisdom of this world, there is indeed no such thing as a free lunch. The sooner you learn this, the smarter you will be.

We express this wisdom in a dozen different proverbs and sayings: *"Caveat emptor*—Let the buyer beware." "Don't take any wooden nickels." "A bird in the hand is worth two in the bush." "Beware of him who comes bearing gifts." There are many ways of putting that worldly wisdom, and every language has such sayings.

Now along comes *grace*. What is grace? Very simply, *grace is a free lunch!*

Grace flies in the face of the world's wisdom and most of our worldly experience. It is altogether different from what we have learned to expect from life.

Is it any wonder that we have a hard time understanding grace? Is it any wonder that perhaps not one person in 10 in your church could give a definition of grace, in spite of hearing about it from the pulpit Sunday after Sunday?

Is it any wonder that after two or three years of confirmation a good student will write (it's true—one of mine did):

Grace is what God gives you to obey the Ten Commandments and go to church on Sunday, so that you go to heaven.

Smart student. He knew there was no such thing as a free lunch. He figured grace was something that enabled you to pay your way to lunch in heaven.

Grace is so utterly different from what we normally meet in the world—the world's wisdom and ways of doing things—that most people find it difficult to understand.

One problem is that words change their meanings through the years. When St. Paul's Cathedral in London was completed in 1710, the architect Christopher Wren conducted King Charles II on a tour of the magnificent structure. At the conclusion he asked for the king's opinion. "It's awful!" said the king. Was Sir Christopher disappointed? Not at all! He was delighted with the king's reaction to this culmination of his life's work!

The story makes no sense to us, because the meaning of the word *awful* has changed. But in the 1700s King Charles meant "awe-full . . . full of awe . . . awe-inspiring." What a difference it makes when a word shifts meaning!

The fact of the matter is that *grace*, in its biblical sense, is no longer a word in our everyday English language. Today we use the word in two ways. *Grace* is a girl's name. *Grace* is the little prayer one says before meals.

We do use two words similar to *grace*, but they also have taken on new meanings over the years. *Graceful* usually means an elegance of movement, such as "a graceful dancer." *Gracious* normally defines a pleasant and congenial behavior in society, such as "a gracious hostess." Of all the *grace* words in English, *gracious* comes the closest to the meaning of the biblical word *grace*, but it doesn't come nearly close enough.

What is worse, not only is the *word* missing from our everyday English language, but the *experience* of grace is contrary to most of our everyday life experiences. We hear about grace on Sundays, but Monday through Friday we know very well that there is no such thing as a free lunch!

What makes this subject so desperately important is that the whole Christian gospel centers on grace. If you do not understand the meaning of grace, you really do not understand the meaning of Christianity. Grace is so central to Christian life that if you misunderstand it a little bit, you will misunderstand Christianity.

Pastors preach about grace a great deal and then are frustrated when people do not seem to grasp its meaning. Pastors know what grace is, because for them it is an "in" word. But just as physicians, lawyers, auto mechanics, plumbers, carpenters, geologists, and other professions use vocabulary which the general public does not understand, so *grace* has become for theologians a technical term which has virtually disappeared from public usage. We have a problem: one of our most important Christian words is not very understandable these days!

The delightful message of grace is that we are held fast in God's hand. The title of this book comes from a small but beautiful marble statue in the Metropolitan Museum of Art in New York City. Auguste Rodin, one of the greatest sculptors of all time, was fond of sculpting hands. Toward the end of the last century, he fashioned a hand which held the clay from which emerges a man and woman. He entitled it *The Hand of God*, and it portrays the creative and "gracious" touch and embrace with which God holds us. The statue was a favorite theme of Rodin and was sculpted several times by him and his students.

When I walk into our own church sanctuary, I look up high above the altar and see a hand sculpted in stone, reaching down out of the sun's rays and clouds. It too is the hand of God, symbolizing God's creative power reaching downward to us.

How can I know that this immensely powerful creative hand which rules the universe is the same hand that holds me with such tenderness and love?

That is what this book is about.

2

Do You Always Get What You Deserve?

"There is no such thing as a free lunch" means, "You get what you deserve." From the time you are born, that fact will be drummed into your life's experience. The lessons start early.

If you are naughty, you will be spanked or punished. You deserve it.

If you study hard, you will get good grades. Play around and you will flunk. Get good grades, and you might get a scholarship. If so, you deserved it. Get poor grades, and you do not deserve a scholarship.

Brush your teeth, and you will avoid cavities. Do not brush, and you deserve those painful trips to the dentist.

Overeat, and you will become—and deserve to become—fat.

We tell our children, "Don't go outside in this weather without overshoes, hat, scarf, and mittens, or you'll catch cold." Then when they catch cold we are tempted to say, "See, I told you so. You deserved it!"

Do your best to prepare and apply for a job, and you might get it. Write a messy application, arrive late for the job interview chewing gum and looking dissheveled, and you probably will not be hired. You get what you deserve.

Put your best efforts into a job, and you will likely move up the ladder of success. Come in late, work sloppily, take half-hour coffee breaks, and you will be fired. Either way, you had it coming.

If you want to do *anything* well, you had better practice it, whether it be giving a speech, performing music, playing on an athletic team, cooking a meal, or doing home repairs. It all comes down to that same bit of wisdom: you get what you deserve!

Even when you pull a sneaky one and get away with something with a boss, friend, or teacher, in your own heart you know the truth: you really deserved to "catch it," but you got away with something.

Again and again, in every field of life that message is hammered home: you get what you deserve. We parents find ourselves telling our children that until our voices are hoarse. After all, we want to prepare them for the "real world," don't we?

We might describe this in terms of fair play. One student works hard, gives a good report, writes a fine paper, hands in a good notebook, and gets a C. Another student does not do as well but gets an A, and you find out the teacher is a good friend of the second student's family. You say, "That's not fair!" Why? Because both those students *should get what they deserve*, shouldn't they? Teachers, coaches, employers, and parents should be fair and give people what they deserve.

That is the way the world is. That is the way the world *ought to be,* isn't it? What kind of a world would we have if teachers handed out grades on the basis of how they liked the color of the students' eyes? Or if a coach liked players with brown hair better than those with black or blond? Or if an employer hired a new secretary because she was gorgeous, even if she could not type? Or if a judge declared innocent an admitted criminal just because they were friends in the same grade school?

Does it not make good sense that people should be rewarded for working hard and doing well? A fine mess we would be in if we did not play fair and give people what they deserve!

Furthermore, it is *so easy* to think the same about God. If a person tries moderately hard to be a good Christian, he or she deserves to be saved and go to heaven, right? Go to church now and then, try to be nice to others, give some to the United Way, and be on a few committees for the community welfare, and you deserve a pat on the back from God, right?

There is a technical term for that kind of thinking— *work righteousness.* That means you are righteous or saved by your works, what you do. Do this and do that, and you will be acceptable in God's sight.

It fits right in with our experience in the rest of life: you get what you deserve, so it is only fair that if you give God a nod or two in his direction, he will be on your side.

In *Tramp Abroad* Mark Twain recalls an incident from his boyhood, when he worked in a Missouri printing shop. A 16-year-old lad named Nicodemus Dodge came in to apply for a job. The editor asked what church

Nicodemus belonged to, and the boy admitted he didn't belong to any church.

"What is your religion?"

"Well, boss, you've kind o' got me thar—and yit you hain't got me so mighty much, nuther. I think 't if a feller he'ps another feller when he's in trouble, and don't cuss, and don't do no mean things, nur noth'n' he ain' no business to do, and don't spell the Saviour's name with a little g, he ain't runnin' no resks—he's about as saift as if he b'longed to a church...."

"But suppose he did spell it with a little g—what then?"

"Well, if he done it a-purpose, I reckon he wouldn't stand no chance—he oughtn't to have no chance, anyway, I'm most rotten certain 'bout that."

Here was a boy street-wise in the ways of the world, and he just carried it over into religion. If you did all those things, you are "safe," that is, okay with God. (Just make doubly sure you spell God with a capital G!)

We run into this mentality all the time. The best place to hear work-righteousness talk is to listen to people at funerals. There you hear such well-meaning comments as:

"She was a wonderful lady, one of the nicest persons I ever knew. If anybody makes it to heaven, she will."

"He was one of our most faithful church members, on about every board and committee we have, and one of our biggest givers too. God will take good care of him."

"With all that suffering she went through, you can be sure that she is at peace with God now."

Those comments sound innocent enough, and certainly their intention is to express affection and appreciation. But listen again, and you will hear that behind

them is the basic view that this person *deserved* to go
to heaven. "They deserve it—it's only fair." Right in line
with the wisdom of this world! They certainly are not
asking for a free lunch. They lived a good life on earth,
so it is only right that they go to heaven. No word about
grace in any of those comments!

In the midst of this worldly way of thinking, which
affects all of us because that is the way we *must* operate
in the world, along comes this thing we call grace.

Grace is something you cannot deserve. It is given—
not because we deserve it, but because the giver wants
to give it. The gift does not depend on anything you are,
or anything you do, or anything you deserve. It depends
solely on the character of the giver.

Grace staggers our minds, because it flies in the face
of all the worldly wisdom we have been accumulating
since our earliest childhood glimmering of "what's fair."
It goes against the grain of everything we have learned
and experienced over the years. Even when somebody
does speak to us of grace, it sounds suspicious, because,
after all, we know "you get what you deserve. That's
only fair!"

There is one exception to the wisdom and practice
of this world, one great big exception. *Love.*

When I came into this world on the morning of March
23, 1935, I did nothing at all to deserve my parents' love.
One might love somebody because he or she is beautiful
and thus "deserves" to be loved, or is at least easy to
love. But my mother recalls that I entered the world
red and wrinkled like a prune, with a head the shape
of a football. No, I did not deserve to be loved for any
handsome good looks. Nor did I make my parents' life

any easier. On the contrary, I deprived them of sleep at all hours of the night. Before I arrived, they could travel with a suitcase or two. With me there, it took a trunk full of nursery equipment. Those of you who have had children know the story well.

But they loved me. Not because of anything in me, but because of something in them. I did not deserve it. For me it was indeed a free lunch!

Some years later I was married, and our own children arrived. My wife and I did not look at the wee bundles in the hospital nursery and ask ourselves if we should love them. We just did. They cried at frightfully inconvenient times, but we loved them. Even when one of them with a pouting lower lip spit out in childish spite, "I don't like you anymore, daddy"—yes, even then we smiled and loved them. It was exhausting staying all those hours next to hospital beds, but we held a hand there, because we loved them.

Deserve love? Love does not ask such foolish questions. It is the very deepest nature of love that it is undeserved.

I am a parish pastor, and I have seen love in action many times. I remember an elderly Norwegian woman with a heart large as Boundary Waters canoe country. When anyone was sick, she was there, and when illness left a vacant store, she spent countless hours there filling in. When our congregation elected her to oversee our shut-in visitation program, she undertook to visit and learn to know every one of our shut-ins—no little task in a large congregation. During her three-year term she was practically another pastor on our staff, and when her term expired she stayed right in touch with the many people she had become concerned about.

There was no question of anybody deserving that kind of love. They all received it because her heart was full of love.

I could tell stories of undeserving love for pages and pages. In times of sickness or difficulty I have seen people rally around with hot dishes, calls, cards, prayers, and concern. Just a few hours before writing this paragraph, I offered the use of the church refrigerator and freezer to a recently widowed woman and her daughter, because so many friends and neighbors had brought food to their house. All this happened not because anybody "deserved" it, but because there was love in many hearts, and that love responded.

We can, of course, be coldly skeptical about love. Strictly speaking, there is probably no such thing as "perfect love" on this earth. Dig hard enough, I suppose, and one can always find some trace of self-interest. We love our children, but there is also some pride of possession. When we fall in love, are there not qualities that make the other person "lovable"? When we do works of love, does there not lurk some little satisfaction at being admired for them, or some hope that they will be returned? Surely, one can be rightfully skeptical about love, because none of us is perfect.

But love still remains the grandest accomplishment we humans have going for us. It does bring out the best of what we can be. It is the one huge exception to the "you-get-what-you-deserve" syndrome of human life.

And once we know something about love, we can begin to understand grace, because love is the closest human thing to grace.

3

What Is Grace and Where Does It Come From?

If it is true that in this world we tend to get what we deserve, and if it is true that love is one exception, then we should ask: where does this love come from?

That brings us to God. The simple Bible verse says it: "God is love" (1 John 4:8). The one primary characteristic of God is that he loves. He loves not because we are lovable and deserving, but because it is his nature to love. He loves even that which is not at all lovable.

I have my confirmation classes memorize 1 John 4:10-11, because those verses put love in perspective and summarize the whole Christian message:

In this is love, not that we loved God but that he loved us and sent his Son to be the expiation for our sins. Beloved, if God so loved us, we also ought to love one another.

If this is too long and the word "expiation" too complicated for some, I have gone to the next paragraph and settled for 1 John 4:19, which says it even more briefly: "We love, because he first loved us."

Another verse we all memorize is that standard favorite, John 3:16. It is a favorite because God's love is right up front, from which everything else follows: "For God so loved the world that he gave his only Son . . . ."

That is grace—the love of God which reaches out to us. In short: grace is what God is!

In the Old Testament there are two words which describe this love of God. The Hebrew word *chen* originally meant "to bend down," as God "bends down" to us. The word *hesed* describes God's loyalty and love to his people, the steadfast love God shows to the people of Israel as he restores them again and again after they have drifted away from him.

The writers of the New Testament took the Greek word *charis* to describe this special quality of God. *Charis* originally meant charm, congeniality, sweetness, kindness, and helpfulness. But in the New Testament that little word took on the grandeur of God's unswerving faithfulness and his constant, undeserved love.

So *love* and *grace* are the two sides of the same coin. Interestingly, when the King James Bible translators needed a word to translate *agape*, the highest form of love in Greek, they used *charity*, a word related to *charis* or grace. So *grace* and *love* are intermingled, both the very heart of God. *Grace* tells us what kind of special, wonderful *love* God has for us!

Love today is a huge word, spreading out from the "Tom Loves Mary" cut into the bark of a tree and the romantic slush in Hollywood magazines, all the way to the indescribable tenderness of parents for their children. *Love* is such a big word that it needs definition, and *grace* is the definition of God's love for us. It is undeserved and unshakable love. Overcome with this wonder, St. Paul interrupts the flow of his letter to the Romans and stumbles all over himself in listing everything he can think of that cannot stop God from loving us:

> For I am sure that neither death, nor life, nor angels, nor principalities, nor things present, nor things to come, nor powers, nor height, nor depth, [and then, just in case he has forgotten anything] nor *anything else in all creation*, will be able to *separate us from the love of God* in Christ Jesus our Lord! (Rom. 8:38-39, italics added).

In his explanation of the First Article of the Apostles' Creed, Martin Luther made certain that we would not confuse the love and grace of God with our worldly mentality of *deserving* what we get: "All this he does out of fatherly and divine goodness and mercy, *though I do not deserve it.*"

Another term often used for *grace* in church history is the Latin *favor*, which meant "unmerited favor." Even today "favor" has the connotation of doing something for somebody out of the goodness of one's heart. But we have corrupted that word by using it in the framework of deserving: "You owe me a favor, because I did something for you," or the saying, "One favor *deserves* another."

Do you want to know what grace is? Dictionary definitions cannot do the job. Grace, like love, is a living thing. To understand it, you must see it or experience it in action. The best place to start is to see it at work in the life of Jesus.

I have seen grace defined on banners as "*G*od's *R*eward *A*t *C*hrist's *E*xpense" or "*G*od's *R*iches *A*t *C*hrist's *E*xpense." Both versions are handy ways to remember what grace is, since the life of Jesus is God's grace written large in human life. The banners can be misleading, however, if we take them to mean that God was an angry and rejecting God until Jesus settled the score. God did not change his mind because of Jesus. God in his grace sent Jesus. Remember John 3:16. Christina Rosetti saw it correctly when she entitled her Christmas hymn "Love Came Down at Christmas."

One interesting thing about the word *charis* in the New Testament is that Jesus never used it. He *embodied* it, and he *lived* it. He *was* God's grace for us. His whole person and ministry were flooded with grace.

What is the parable of the Prodigal Son (or Waiting Father) but a story of grace? The father whose son has squandered half of the family wealth still waits longingly each day for the boy to come home, rushing out to receive him with an embrace when the lad finally does return (Luke 15:11-24).

The parable of the Good Samaritan is another story of grace. The Samaritan was good because he aided a battered traveler who not only did not deserve his assistance, but who never would have dreamed that a halfbreed Samaritan would have stopped by to help (Luke 10:30-37).

Consider the people whose lives Jesus touched. It is grace again and again. Zacchaeus, the crooked tax collector, only wanted to see Jesus, but he discovered his whole life changed when Jesus invited himself to dinner

(Luke 19:1-10). Matthew's entire life took a radical turn when Jesus looked at him and said, "Follow me" (Matt. 9:9). The woman taken in adultery expected to be crushed in a hail of rocks, but she heard Jesus say only, "Neither do I condemn you; go, and do not sin again" (John 8:11). One after another in the Gospels we read of people whose lives were touched by grace—by Jesus' life.

Then came the end, when, amidst the ghastly pain of crucifixion, he looked out over the crowd of hateful and jeering faces contorted with anger, and he gasped out those words which nobody would expect a human being ever to say in that situation: "Father, forgive them; for they know not what they do" (Luke 23:34).

It was grace, all grace!

We already know that *love* is one excellent word which helps to understand grace. Another helpful word is *acceptance.* A person might not know what grace is, but every one of us knows what acceptance is, and we all long for it.

Every one of us has felt like an outsider sometime, standing lonely as all the others seemed to be enjoying themselves. Every one of us has felt the sting of rejection, whether deserved or not. Every one of us has behaved badly and been criticized, or shunned, and known that we had it coming.

"To be accepted"—what a wonderful sound that phrase has!

Think of a boy who dreams of making the football team. After doing his best in preseason practices, nothing in all the world is so sweet to him as seeing his name on the team roster and having the other players clap him on the back and say, "Good to have you on the team!"

Or imagine a girl who has spent a great deal of time during high school envying the really popular girls and is now worried that no one will ask her to the prom. Finally a boy calls her, the boy she has hoped might like her, and invites her to go with him. The night arrives, and as he walks out the door with her, he takes her hand in his and says, "You're beautiful tonight." *That* is acceptance, and it floods the heart with joy!

The fairy tale "Cinderella" has such eternal appeal because there is a universal longing for acceptance. Poor little Cinderella lives under the carping criticism of her spiteful stepmother and dreadful sisters. But her fairy godmother enables her to attend the ball, where the handsome young prince has eyes only for her, falls in love with her and searches the entire kingdom until he finds her again. She has been rejected all her life, but the prince accepts her, and her dreams come true!

It is the same theme in Hans Christian Andersen's story "The Ugly Duckling." The homely little bird is laughed at and ridiculed by the other ducks. But he grows into a beautiful swan, and everybody oohs and aahs at how marvelous a bird he is. He is accepted.

Acceptance is a wonderful thing. Each one of us would shrivel up in despair if we did not experience it.

And yet there is a difference between these two stories about acceptance and what we read about in the Bible. Cinderella and the ugly duckling really *deserve* to be accepted. Cinderella really *was* the loveliest and nicest girl in the kingdom. The problem was that her stepmother and stepsisters kept her cooped up by the fireplace. Once she got to the ball, everyone saw how beautiful she was. The prince's love was not really an act of grace in the biblical sense. He was just smart enough to recognize the best-looking girl!

It is the same with the ugly duckling. Had the ducks accepted the ugly bird, *that* would have been grace. But they did not. The duckling was not accepted until he deserved it, after he had become the finest-looking bird in the pond.

Acceptance is wonderful, but grace is acceptance on a much higher level: grace is acceptance when it is undeserved. We are not accepted because of who we are—lovely Cinderellas or elegant swans. We are accepted because of what God *is*, that is, *grace-full*. He loves us and accepts us even as we remain imperfect. Paul stresses this key aspect of grace:

> For when we were still helpless, Christ died for the wicked at the time that God chose. It is a difficult thing for someone to die for a righteous person. It may be that someone might dare to die for a good person. But God has shown us how much he loves us—*it was while we were still sinners* that Christ died for us! (Rom. 5:6-8 TEV, italics added).

In our congregation we are fond of showing a movie about a handsome Polynesian fellow named Johnny Lingo, who is looking for a wife. Everyone is speculating about which lucky girl he will select. Finally he surprises everyone by picking Mahana, a shy, rather plain girl. He goes to Mahana's father to bargain about the dowry. The neighbors gossip that the father will accept almost any offer, maybe even just one cow, to get his homely daughter off his hands. They are astonished when the greedy father announces the price: "Three cows!" They know Johnny can get much more attractive girls for less. But they gasp again when Johnny insists on giving no less than *eight cows* for his bride. "Let everyone know," he says, "that Johnny Lingo's wife is worth far more than just one, two, or even three cows!" The handsome groom and happy wife are married and sail off on their honeymoon trip.

Some time later the two return. No longer is the girl plain. She is radiantly beautiful. It is the same girl, but for the past months she has lived in the wonder of being loved by someone who accepted her, loved her and thought she was worth far more than anybody else had thought or even than she had dared believe or hope.

That was grace. It was undeserved love and acceptance, and it conveyed the power to transform her.

Grace is a funny thing. You cannot talk about grace much without getting a smile on your face and a bounce in your heart. Grace is funny because it is ridiculous and because it is joyful.

First, it is ridiculous. It is a funny thing that God comes to us with a message that violates all our worldly common sense. Why should he be gracious—he, the majestic Lord and Creator of the universe, who can order and command justice and obedience from all his creation? But he lays all that majesty aside, takes the punishment of sin upon himself through Jesus, and waves us all home free. Then he looks at me, pronounces me "righteous," and there I find myself, lined up with all the royal saints in the kingdom of heaven. Yet I know, and he knows, that I am still a sinner. He has involved me in a kind of heavenly joke, treating sinful me as a righteous person. Funny business, isn't it?

The apostle Paul had a hard time persuading his readers to take him seriously about this grace. He discovered that the reaction of any thinking person to this message was: "Look, if you aren't saved by what you do, but by God's grace, why not go out and sin all over the place?" Or some had even a better line: "If God gives you enough grace to cover all your sins, then why not sin a whole lot more, to receive a whole lot more grace?" (Rom. 6). That does make some sense, doesn't it? But grace is something different from the way we think about things. Paul freely admits that the grace of God is different from earthly wisdom and that grace might strike a worldly-wise person as foolishness. "It pleased God through the folly of what we preach to save those who believe" (1 Cor. 1:21; see the whole section, 1 Cor. 1:17-31).

Second, grace is joyful. Here I am sinful, and I ought to be frightfully worried about my sins as I stand before a perfect God. But as I get down on my knees, he pulls me upright and says, "Welcome to my kingdom and my people. Now you're a saint!" My instinct is to think, "Come on, God, you're kidding me!" I am puzzled by it all, but it is surely wonderful news!

What possible reaction can we have but joy? We are so accustomed to hearing this terrific good news that we listen to sermons with inappropriately straight faces! If a minister were to preach a sermon to people who were hearing this gospel for the very first time, a more fitting reaction would be at least to smile at the wonder of it all and maybe break out with a "Hurrah!" A Christian might face all kinds of suffering and tragedy during life, but the undercurrent of all Christian life is joy, thanks to grace. What a splendid title Edna Hong picked for her book about grace—*The Gayety of Grace*!

Why is it that we human beings so often succeed in clouding over the joy of grace and make the Christian life something so dreadfully grim? Look at the gloom of the medieval age, the fractious and bitter theological battles of the Reformation, the depressing glumness of the Puritans, and the lack of enjoyment in the lives of many of today's overly religious types!

But put grace back in the middle, where it belongs, and one cannot help but find real joy!

4

What Went Wrong?

We need grace because there is something terribly haywire here on earth. What is it? Since we do not have a word like *ungrace*, we shall just call it *sin*, because sin is the opposite of grace.

What is sin? If grace is self-giving and unselfish, then sin is self-serving and selfish. And that is precisely what went wrong with the world.

To understand what sin is, we need only go back and look at the beginning. The account in Genesis 3 does not only describe the first sin. It describes the very nature of sin.

"We may eat the fruit of any tree in the garden," the woman answered, "except the tree in the middle of it. God told us not to eat the fruit of that tree or even touch it. If we do, we will die."

The snake replied, "That's not true; you will not die. God said that because he knows that when you eat it, you will be like God . . . ."

> The woman saw how beautiful the tree was and how good its fruit would be to eat, and she thought how wonderful it would be to become wise (Gen. 3:2-6 TEV).

What a clever serpent! He said, "How would you like to become as smart as God? Why not put yourself in God's place?" That was the temptation that did it.

Self-centeredness, pride, egoism—that's what sin is—just the opposite of grace, which gives of itself for the other. One must have love of self, self-respect, and self-esteem to be healthy, but sin is self gone amok, the self elevated above others and above even God.

Occasionally I do an experiment with my confirmation class. I hand out sections of the newspaper and ask students to pick out a story that illustrates how self-centeredness causes problems in the world. Some get the front page, others the business section or sport section. Some complain that they were given only the comics or movie sections. (Soon they realize that those are the easiest.) It is not long before they find good examples: labor strikes where each side wants its level of pay and benefits, quarrels between nations, all manner of crime in which the criminal victimizes somebody for money or revenge, comics that display selfishness, "Dear Ann" and "Dear Abby" which are full of problems of self-centeredness, accidents caused by somebody driving as fast as he wants instead of a safer speed for others. Turn the pages yourself, and you can find plenty of such examples.

It's the sin of Adam and Eve—"me first!"—that's what's wrong with the world.

Look at movies and television for more examples. Westerns are a gold mine of illustrations. Ranchers move on land, so Indians burn farms, so cowboys shoot a couple of Indians, so Indians burn whole villages, so cowboys massacre a lot of Indians, and so on.

Revenge has a way of getting worse with each step. If somebody shoves you, you shove back, but a little harder. Then he hits you, and you hit back harder, and then he jumps you, and there is a full-scale brawl. It is the age-old human story.

Occasionally somebody will say to me, "I have a hard time believing in 'original sin.' " The term is puzzling, but in fact original sin is the one doctrine in the Christian faith which even non-Christians might well agree with just by looking around at the state of the world! It is "the sin of our origin," the sin that is within us even as we are born, or that condition we are born into that will result inevitably in our being sinful. Original sin means that at no age in my life can I say, "Everyone else around here is sinful, but I'm not going to sin at all." No human being could do that. Even if one could say that and carry it off, he or she has already sinned before knowing enough to speak a sentence like that.

After my newspaper exercise I often ask my confirmation class at what age they think sin begins. I ask at what age they may have detected sin in younger brothers and sisters. They always agree that their younger family members are little sinners. After thinking about it, they usually agree that at least by age three or four there is ample evidence of sin.

We remind ourselves what sin is—self-centeredness and selfishness—and then we consider even babies. Who is more self-centered and selfish than a tiny baby? What baby waits patiently for his or her parents' usual waking hour to cry for breakfast? What baby waits until mother has finished her phone conversation to yell a complaint about a messy diaper? No, a baby has only one thing in mind: *me, my* comfort!

Of course it is nonsense to speak of this as sinning. At that stage it is survival. Furthermore, those periods of infant and childhood development that we parents find the most difficult—such as the "terrible twos"—are necessary for a child to grow toward a sense of self.

But this childhood characteristic does give us a tip-off on how this little human will develop. Most toddlers learn the word *mine* as soon as they learn *mama*. Watch a toddler with six toys, more than he can possibly play with, and take one away! We have all seen a child start playing with another child's toy only to have the owner—to the mother's horror—swing and clout the borrower. There you have on the smallest scale what world wars are made of!

The point is that every one of us is born with that condition which will lead inescapably to sinning. It is there at our very origin: "original sin."

How does one break this downward spiral of sin, where pride and selfishness get worse and more destructive? By grace. Somebody has to say, "I for one am not going to continue this back-and-forth revenge. I am going to quit it." Once one side quits, the other side may find it pointless to continue. If somebody shoves you and you do not shove back—a hard thing to restrain, since all our natural instincts are to strike back—there may not be any fight at all. It is grace Jesus recommends in the Sermon on the Mount:

"You have heard it was said: 'An eye for an eye, and a tooth for a tooth.' But now I tell you: do not take revenge on someone who does you wrong. If anyone slaps you on the right cheek, let him slap your left cheek too (Matt. 5:38-39 TEV).

Difficult advice, isn't it? But nobody ever said grace was easy.

Sydney J. Harris entitled one of his columns "Friends Are to Be 'Put Up' With":

A couple I know slightly stopped seeing another couple who were their closest friends. It seems that the second couple turned up two hours late to an important dinner the first couple were giving.

"You simply don't treat good friends that way," said the hostess, who was filled with wrongeous indignation. "I won't put up with that sort of thing.

Mr. Harris correctly observes:

But this is exactly what good friends are for—to put up with. Friendship, of the true sort, means accepting another person, not for his good points, but in spite of his bad points.

There you have a classic example of sin and grace. The first paragraphs illustrate sin: if a person offends me or slights me, I bristle with indignation. I have been wronged, and I get even. I lash back more severely than the offense even warrants. In this case the hostess so overreacted that she wrecked the whole friendship. There's a downward spiral! The third paragraph tells how grace enters the picture: "accepting another person, not for his good points, but in spite of his bad points."

Have you known people who are so supersensitive that they become angry at their friends, one by one, until they really haven't any friends left? It is indeed a sad sight. It is sin, carried too far.

Some centuries ago theologians used a Latin term to describe what sin is: *incurvatus in se*, "curved in upon oneself." In colloquial English we call it "navel gazing." Sin is self-centeredness, pride, and egoism—a preoccupation with myself. This is the root of all sin, and as long as I am *incurvatus* in myself, I will inevitably sin.

How can this grip be broken? Do I avoid the sin of too much pride by going to the other extreme and considering myself worthless? Not at all! Protestantism has been plagued by what a friend of mine labeled "worm theology," that is, a morbid view that we resist the sin of pride by belittling, even hating, ourselves. We now know that a healthy self-respect is necessary for every human being. If we do not love or like ourselves, we shall become depressed, neurotic, or vulnerable to some other disorder. When Jesus said, "Love your neighbor as yourself," he was assuming that we do love ourselves.

The answer is neither in "curving in" upon myself nor in considering myself worthless, but in seeing myself as part of a larger picture. When we become interested and centered in something or somebody other than ourselves we cease being focused exclusively on ourselves as Number One. Then something strange happens: my concern for that other person or persons shifts my total attention away from me, and I am able to give myself to others.

That is grace: giving of oneself for some other or others.

Murdo Macdonald, a well-known Scottish Presbyterian preacher and professor of preaching in Glasgow, once told an American audience that he learned more about grace from his comrades in the Second World War than from his theological teachers. When he entered the British armed forces, he was, in his own words, "a kind of prig, a bit moralistic and over-puritanical." The event which "liberated me more than anything that ever happened to me," was when a fellow soldier was badly wounded by a shell fragment that ripped a gaping hole through his neck. It was clear that medical help would never arrive in time. As Captain Macdonald cradled his dying friend's head in his lap, the man tried to speak, but the air escaping from the horrible wound and the lack of control of his tongue made speaking difficult. Leaning forward and straining to understand, Macdonald finally made out the words: "I'm alright, sir, you take care of yourself." The force of these words was so powerful that in that instant Macdonald knew he was seeing grace in action. Here was a man, dying in agony, who thought first of the safety of his friend!

It is the opposite of *incurvatus in se*, and only grace can counteract the toxic venom of self-centered sin which poisons our world.

Only by shifting the focus of our life out beyond ourselves can this grip of self-centeredness be broken. When that does happen, a person is transformed. A fundamental change takes place in that person's perspective and whole life.

George Eliot's novel *Silas Marner* used to be standard reading in high school. Remember that shriveled-up old miser Silas? Falsely accused of stealing, the bitter weaver lived for 15 years as a recluse. His only interest in life was to take out his hoard of gold at night and let the shining pieces run through his fingers. One night even that was stolen from him by a ransacking burglar, and his life was shattered. Then one New Year's Eve a destitute woman left her little blond girl sleeping in front of the fireplace in Silas' cottage, and the next day Silas found the mother's dead body a short distance from the cottage.

Nobody claimed the child, so she lived with the miser. Slowly the old man fell under the spell of the irrepressibly cheerful child. The delight of caring for the golden-haired girl gradually caused him to forget his lost gold, and as she moved happily among the villagers he too was drawn from his shell and began to speak again with his neighbors. The cottage took on a new appearance, with lacy curtains decorating the once drab windows.

Silas was happy. There was light in his eyes, a smile on his face, affection in his voice, and a bounce to his step. He was no longer "curved in upon himself." The focus of his life had shifted outside of himself, to little Eppie. He had re-entered the human race. In biblical language, he had been touched by grace, because he had given himself to someone else.

Grace is the only thing that can work this miracle, on whatever level it occurs. The only thing that can break this crust of selfishness and pride is grace, for grace is that quality which sees beyond itself and gives of itself to others.

Where can we find grace? We look to God, from whom it comes in the first place.

5

Who Am I?

In *The Lonely Crowd*, David Riesman contrasts two types of personalities—the "inner-directed" and the "outer-directed" persons. Outer-directed persons depend for identity and guidance on people around them. They do well when those around them are accepting and affirming. But when they sense disapproval and criticism from others, their self-confidence and ability to perform wobble. Inner-directed persons, on the other hand, have a secure enough identity within themselves, so that they can stand up even amidst criticism and speak their own mind or maintain their composure. The direction for their lives is given by their own inner convictions. They are not controlled by the whims of public opinion.

Naturally we all wanted to see ourselves as inner-directed. And of course the mark of maturity in human beings is that we do develop this inner gyroscope within ourselves—a healthy self-respect and a sense of purpose in life—so that we are not dependent upon others.

But as much as we would like to think of ourselves as inner-directed, we are affected by other people around us. When we are close to other people, we cannot help but be sensitive to what they think of us, and that does affect our self-image.

It begins in childhood. A child who grows up with loving parents will feel that love. If the parents give that child little affection and much criticism and rejection, that child's self-image will be scarred. When we sense love from family and friends, we feel good about ourselves. When others reject us, we cannot help but feel our own self-worth in question.

It is a matter of balance. As we grow older and more mature, we develop our own inner identity and sense of self-worth, so that we can function even when we meet with disapproval. We can be inner-directed. But we can never—nor would we want to—be so isolated from sensitive relationships with other people that we would be invulnerable to their feelings and opinions about us.

When we perceive people to be inner-directed, we tend to say, "Yes, they really know who they are."

Who am I? This is one of the most urgent questions we ask ourselves, particularly in our growing years as we grope for our own "identity." Even 400 years before Christ the wisest man in ancient Greece, Socrates, gave us his famous advice, "Know thyself."

A mark of maturity is to have a sense of "who I am." That identity comes from the circumstances surrounding me as I grow up.

I am a member of my family. My identity includes years of wonderful memories from my family as I grew up. (It also includes the memory of times I was spanked and the times I, regrettably now, was not very nice to my brothers and sister!) I love to listen to and retell stories of my grandparents and my immigrant great-grandparents who came from Norway, because all that is part of my identity.

I am proud to be an American. That too is my identity. But I also have special feelings about other countries. I am proud that part of my identity is tied to the country of Hungary, because my wife was born there. Since I have lived in Germany and France, those countries too are part of who I am.

My identity is intertwined with schools I have attended, people I have known, experiences I have had, and the opinions I have formed.

But there is the larger picture too. In Thornton Wilder's play *Our Town* the first act closes as 11-year-old Rebecca Gibbs is looking out the window at the moon with her 16-year-old brother George, musing about where else in the world the moon might be shining at that same moment. We hear the following conversation:

REBECCA: I never told you about that letter Jane Crofut got from her minister when she was sick . . . . He wrote Jane a letter and on the envelope the address was like this: It said: Jane Crofut; The Crofut Farm; Grover's Corners; Sutton County; New Hampshire; United States of America.

GEORGE: What's funny about that?

REBECCA: But listen, it's not finished: the United States of America; Continent of North America; Western Hemisphere; the Earth; the Solar System; the Universe; the Mind of God—that's what it said on the envelope.

GEORGE: What do you know!

REBECCA: And the postman brought it just the same.

GEORGE: What do you know!

That too is part of our identity—the larger picture. How do you identify yourself? Do you stop with the country, "America"? Do you see yourself as a "citizen of planet earth"? And finally: Is your identity traced back to "the Mind of God"?

If God is part of your identity, then you are linked with the Creator and Lord of the whole creation.

But it makes a great deal of difference how God forms your identity. If you see God as a fierce and unremitting judge, then you live in fear in the depths of your being. If you understand God as a rather impersonal "force" or "being," too big to be interested in you, then your identity will not be shaped much by him at all. But if God is for you a loving parent, then your identity will be based on the conviction that the great God and Creator of all things loves you!

That is an enormously solid and unshakable foundation for one's identity! It means that no matter who does or does not like me, God Almighty does love me. Even if *everybody* around me rejects me, it would be a painful experience, but I can grasp tight to the knowledge that the great God of all things loves me. No matter what tragedies and hardships might rock my identity, at the center of my being is the faith and trust that God loves me. I might even feel my sanity slipping away, or be dogged by depression or other mental illnesses, but I hope that I would retain the trust that God still loves me in spite of all.

It is this faithfulness of God written about in the Old Testament that has given the Jews their identity and sustained them all these years. We Christians add the tangible love of God we see in Jesus through the New Testament. The gospel of the loving God is indeed the rock on which our identity is established.

If we worry that we do not love God as we should, even that does not alter the foundation of our identity, because *nothing*, not "anything else in all creation will be able to separate us from the love of God in Christ Jesus our Lord" (Rom. 8:39). Samuel Johnson, the English writer of the late 1700s, penned a little ditty about a Mr. Crowe, who apparently had boasted about his lack of faith:

> We've heard in language highly spiced
> That Crowe does not believe in Christ.
> But what we're more concerned to know
> Is whether Christ believes in Crowe!

That is indeed the great truth: Christ does believe in Crowe!

In short, our identity is based—on grace!

Who am I? First and foremost, I am a person loved by God. No matter who else might love me or not love me, no matter what my accomplishments or lack of them might be, that great affirmation fixes my identity in the very greatest sense possible, for God is above all.

Lilly Langtry was a beauty who took Edwardian London by storm toward the end of the last century. No less than the Prince of Wales was her suitor, and the public clamored to see her perform in London theaters.

On one transatlantic crossing she became acquainted with Somerset Maugham. During a conversation she told the distinguished author that the most celebrated man in two hemispheres was Fred Gebhard.

Surprised, Maugham asked why this Fred Gebhard was so famous.

"Because I loved him," replied the actress.

There is of course a touch of arrogance in that story, but also of truth. Whoever Fred Gebhard was, the one fact that will fix his identity in history is that a very famous actress loved him.

A Christian's identity is fixed because God loves us. Not only our identity, but our worth and our eternal destiny as well. Everything we are and everything we do flows from that ringing affirmation: we live in God's grace!

Peer Gynt was a roguish but charming rascal created by Henrik Ibsen. His is a story about identity and self. As a youngster, Peer could not separate fact from fiction, and his mother Ase never knew if he were telling the truth or fanciful stories. He could never stick to anything very long. He ran off with Ingrid, but soon tired of her and abandoned her. He was willing to join the trolls, but left them when they wanted to change him into one of themselves.

Fleeing from the angry trolls, Peer confronted the mysterious dark force, the *Boyg*, who urged him not to go straight to his goal, but to "go roundabout." That advice reinforced the pattern of Peer's life, for there were no goals, dreams or principles that he pursued with single-minded purpose.

As he grew into adulthood, Peer spoke a great deal about his "self," but the reader realizes that there is no real "self" of any integrity or harmony to Peer at all. He does not stand for anything or see anything through. He made a lot of money shipping slaves to America and idol images to China. But lest anybody think him a heathen, he also sent missionaries and Bibles to China. Although his sentiments were with the Greeks in their war against the Turks, he invested his money with the Turks, because there was more profit on that side.

As an older man he finally wended his way back to Norway. He was proud that he had been "himself," but he did not realize that there had never been a solid "self" to him at all, just whims blowing here and there.

In the depths of a forest, Peer paused to eat wild onions. He took an onion in his hand, musing that this onion might represent himself, and began to peel away each layer, thinking of the layers and experiences of his own life. He looked for the core, which he compared to the core of his life, his "self." Layer after layer he peeled, thinking to himself:

> What an enormous number of layers! Isn't the kernel soon coming to light? (*Pulls the whole onion to pieces.*) I'm blest if it is! To the innermost center it's nothing but layers—each smaller and smaller.

A look of panic crossed his face as the thought struck him that his own life might be that too—layers of experiences with no kernel in the middle!

As he continued to walk, he noticed threadballs rolling at his feet and heard their voices like children weeping, "We are thoughts you should have thought." He saw withered leaves blowing about and heard them saying, "We are the words you should have spoken." He heard sighing in the air, and they said to him, "We are the songs you should have sung, but a thousand times over you have smothered us." Dewdrops dripping from the branches told him, "We are your tears that are unshed. We could have melted sharp wounding, but now the barb rankles." Broken straws moving in the wind said, "We are the deeds you should have performed, but your doubt has crippled us." Peer's "identity" was shown to be nothing but a long series of lost opportunities!

Then Peer met a button molder, who was looking for him. "I'm a button molder," he said, "You're to go into my ladle."

"And what to do there?" Peer asked.

"To be melted down."

"To be melted?" Peer replied. "But this, my good man, is most unfair. I'm sure I deserve better treatment than this. I'm not nearly so bad as perhaps you think—I've done a good deal of good in the world. At worst you may call me a sort of a bungler—but certainly not an exceptional sinner."

"Why, that's precisely the rub, my man," the button molder told him. "You're no sinner at all in the higher sense. That's why you're to land in the casting ladle .... You're not one thing nor the other, only so-so."

Yes, Peer's problem was that he had no identity. He was neither saint nor sinner. He drifted. He had no inner character. So the molder had orders to put him back in the pot, remelt him, and try again. The order read: "Peer Gynt shall you summon .... Clap him into the ladle with other spoiled goods."

Peer became desperate. He could not find anybody who would testify that he amounted to anything, either for good or for evil. The button molder hovered over him with his ladle and melting pot. In panic Peer asked, "What is, at bottom, this 'being yourself'?"

The molder answered, "To stand forth everywhere with the Master's intention displayed like a signboard." Peer had failed. He had never wondered what he was intended to be, never been led by anything larger than his own momentary desires. He cried out for one last chance to prove that he was somebody, that he had an identity.

He rushed to the hut of Solveig, the girl he left behind so many years ago. He called for her to curse him, because leaving her was a despicable thing to do. The button molder waited at the side of the house to hear her condemnation.

But contrary to Peer's expectation she embraced him with joy: "You have made all my life as a beautiful song! Blessed are you for returning!"

Peer pleaded with her, "Say where I have been all these years!"

Solveig smiled. "Oh, that riddle is easy."

Peer urged her again, "Then tell what you know! Where was I, as myself, as the whole man, the true man? Where was I?"

Solveig replied, "In my faith, in my hope, and in my love!"

Peer's face lit up as he realized that he *had* been somebody, in Solveig's heart! He had had an identity, a self, in her love all that time as she waited and longed for him. He cried out, " . . . in your love—oh, there hide me, hide me!" He was safe from the button molder.

Peer's identity was in her love, and it was that love which saved him.

So is our identity in the love of God, and we cry out to him, "In your love, keep me, oh, keep me!"

6

Justified by Grace

A favorite religious type in cartoons is the fellow who accosts people on the street by asking, "Are you saved?"

Salvation or *being saved* are terms often used to describe God's purpose for mankind. It is very interesting to ask a group of people, "What *is* salvation?" What does it mean, "to be saved"? We talk about it, but do we ever stop to think what it is?

What does God have in mind for us? *Salvation* is one word we can use, but the Bible uses many others: justification, reconciliation, redemption, forgiveness, deliverance, transformation, rebirth, renewal, victory over evil, atonement, eternal life.

There is no such thing in the Bible as a theory or doctrine of salvation. The Bible is a record of events—God's encounters with people through the centuries and our responses. In the Bible we find words from all walks of life to describe what happens between God and us. Scottish theologian George Caird put it this way:

The New Testament . . . does not attempt to give any rea-
soned theory of the atonement. Instead it gives us a
series of pictures, which tell us in the language of the
heart what the Cross meant to those who wrote. We
were in debt, and Christ paid our debt for us; we were
slaves, and he gave his life for our ransom; we were
condemned before the judgment seat of God, and he
bore our penalty that we might go free; . . . we were children in disgrace, and he restored us to the family circle;
we were prisoners shut up in the fortress of Satan, and
he broke in to set us free. The terminology of the bank,
the slave market, the law courts, the temple, the home,
and the field of battle is pressed into service in an attempt to do justice to the fact of experience that sin is
no longer a barrier between man and God.

So there are lots of words for salvation. How you
describe it will depend on how you perceive what is
wrong with the human race and what needs correcting.
Or, in personal terms, how you think of salvation will
reflect the state of your own soul and how God meets
you.

If the problem of guilt or sin is uppermost in our
minds, then "forgiveness of sins" will be the first thing
we think about as salvation.

If our separation from God and therefore from our
fellow humans seems to be the main problem, then we
shall emphasize "reconciliation."

If we feel rejected and unacceptable, then "acceptance" will be the dominant theme of salvation.

There are others. If we are facing death, "going to
heaven" will be important for us in describing salvation.
If we are hopelessly confused about how we should
live, then "Jesus' way of life" or "discipleship" will be

salvation for us. If life has no meaning, then we shall see salvation as "the meaning of life." If our problem is a sense of terrible loneliness and alienation, then salvation's main thrust will be "to become a part of the community of the church, the body of Christ."

Perhaps you can think of others. God understands the entire spectrum of human experience, and salvation is whatever way he comes into our lives wherever we are. Whatever the situation, it is God's grace which confronts it.

One of the apostle Paul's favorite words to describe what God has done for us is *justification*—to be *justified*. Paul borrows this legal term from courtroom language: God considers us righteous or "not guilty" on account of what Jesus has done for us.

> ...since all have sinned and fall short of the glory of God, they are justified by his grace as a gift, through the redemption which is in Christ Jesus, whom God put forward as an expiation by his blood, to be received by faith (Rom. 3:23-25).

Justification means that in God's eyes we are just, or righteous. In the imagery of the courtroom God looked down from the judge's bench and would have had to pronounce us guilty, but when he looked down he saw Jesus, who had taken our place in the defendant's chair. Jesus was fully righteous, but he had come to live in our place and he had died, which he would not have had to do. But even more wondrously, death had not been able to claim him, and the tomb of despair on Good Friday became the empty tomb of joy on Easter morning.

In the "Good News for Modern Man" Bible translation (Today's English Version), "justified" is translated
as "put right." In Jesus Christ we can be "justified" or
"put right," and it happens because God is a God of
grace. We are "justified by grace."

You might find yourself in a discussion over which
phrase is correct: "Justified by grace" or "justified by
faith." You could choose the full phrase, "justified by
grace through faith."

Prepositions are slippery little words. You could say,
"I came home by sheer determination last night," or, "I
came home by car last night," or, "I came home by the
east road last night." The word *by* means three slightly
different things: the cause which enabled you to do it,
the means by which you did it, or the route which ac-
complished the goal.

"Justified by grace" or "justified by faith" are both
correct, although *by* is used differently in each phrase.
It is God's grace which saves, or justifies, us. We receive
it by faith, that is *via* or *through* faith. Grace does it,
and grace is channeled through faith.

I like the phrase "justified by grace through faith,"
and I have my confirmation classes memorize Ephesians 2:8-9:

> For by grace you have been saved through faith; and
> this is not your own doing, it is the gift of God—not
> because of works, lest any man should boast.

That keeps things straight, and also tells us exactly
why it is so important: so that we do not get all proud
about being saved. Why should I be proud when pen-
icillin clears up an infection of mine? I can be grateful

to Sir Alexander Fleming and other scientists and the drug company for providing the medicine. I can be grateful to the physician who diagnosed the problem and prescribed the medicine. I can be grateful for the opportunity to work and to pay for the drug. But it would be nonsense for me to say, "What a splendid fellow I am for being cured!"

The only thing I did was to not keep my mouth clamped shut when the spoonful of medicine was given to me. Some people like to make something of this, my contribution to my cure or salvation, but it is such a trifle that the most correct response is to say, "Hurrah! God did it all for me. Thanks be to him!"

Furthermore, in some mysterious way, faith itself is a gift. The whole process of salvation, from beginning to end, is a gift.

I never *decided* to trust my parents. I just did it, early on. I never *decided* to trust my wife. There was just something about her which brought out my trust. It was she that did it, not I. I never really *decide* with my brain to trust anybody or anything. That quality of trustworthiness comes from the person or object being trusted, not from myself. By some strange process that I cannot understand or explain, when I confront and learn to know someone who can be trusted, a trust grows within me. It is not something I do, but something given to me by that quality in the other person.

Faith works something like that. When a sinful person, separated from God, hears the gospel, his or her brain really does not have the capacity to decide on its own whether or not it is true and can be trusted. That trust comes from the gospel itself, and something within responds, "Yes, I trust and believe." It really is impossible to analyze that psychological process any further, except to say that something did make it possible for me to trust, something for which I can take no credit.

What else can it be than God himself? The Word that I hear carries within itself the Spirit of God, which works where the Word is spoken.

Martin Luther summed it up when he explained the Third Article of the Apostles' Creed: "I believe in the Holy Spirit . . ."

> I believe that I cannot by my own understanding or effort believe in Jesus Christ, my Lord, or come to him. But the Holy Spirit has called me through the Gospel, enlightened me with his gifts, and sanctified and kept me in true faith.

In *Wishful Thinking: A Theological ABC* Frederick Buechner writes:

> Grace is something you can never get but only be given. There's no way to earn it or bring it about any more than you can deserve the taste of raspberries and cream or earn good looks or bring about your own birth . . . .
>
> A crucial eccentricity of the Christian faith is the assertion that people are saved by grace. There's nothing *you* have to do. There's nothing you *have* to do. There's nothing you have to *do* . . . .
>
> Like any other gift, the gift of grace can be yours only if you'll reach out and take it.

And then, so we cannot think our "reaching out" in faith is of some credit to us, Mr. Buechner ends by saying: "Maybe being able to reach out and take it is a gift too."

Whether you prefer "justified by grace" or "justified by faith" or "justified by grace through faith," the important thing is that we understand what these phrases intend to say: salvation is 100% from God!

Protestants are supersensitive about this, because the Reformation—that period in the 1500s when most of the Protestant churches were formed—was at its very heart a rediscovery of the gospel of grace. By the 1500s the Roman Catholic Church was enormously powerful. The piety of the people had shifted from trust in grace and the gospel to obedience to the church. Life was grim, and even within the church there was little joy and happiness in being a Christian. Jesus was almost always portrayed in his terrible torment on the cross or as the terrifying judge on judgment day. The general atmosphere in the church was one of fear.

People were preoccupied with the sufferings of purgatory, the "front porch" of heaven where Christians went after death to be "purged" so they would be cleansed enough for heaven. You were destined to spend time in purgatory depending on how much you had sinned. The sufferings of purgatory were depicted in grisly detail, and people clamored to do whatever was necessary to have them diminished or eliminated.

One could escape the hardships of purgatory by gaining an indulgence, which was a reduction or release of the years of suffering your sins had destined you for in purgatory. You gained an indulgence by good works— prayer, pilgrimage, acts of charity, observing relics of saints, or contributing money to the church. Even a little prayer, such as "Jesus, save me. Amen," would take a month off your time in purgatory. A major good work (such as a pilgrimage to Rome or even to Wittenberg, Germany, to see Duke Frederick's collection of relics) would win for you a full or plenary indulgence, that is, immediate elimination of all your time in purgatory. If you died the moment you gained a plenary indulgence, you would go straight to heaven.

This preoccupation with purgatory and indulgences was a perversion of traditional Roman Catholic faith, but it was what existed in central Europe in the early 1500s. In 1517 a Dominican monk, John Tetzel, went about Saxony raising money to build St. Peter's Basilica in Rome by selling indulgences, promising a plenary indulgence to contributors. This so enraged the Augustinian monk and professor of Bible Martin Luther that he wrote a list of 95 statements or theses, protesting this offensive indulgence traffic, and nailed it to the door of the castle church in Wittenberg, inviting other scholars to debate the issue with him.

That issue and other abuses in the church caused Luther and others to dig into their Bibles and rethink the development of Roman Catholic faith and practices over the past centuries. In the years that followed, they concluded that the wonder of the gospel, the message of grace, had been badly obscured. It had been "legalized," made into laws. Obedience to the laws and regulations of the church was in the center, not faith in the gospel, the "good news" of God's grace. Christianity was not liberating but enslaving. Divine punishment was in the forefront, more than God's love. Worst of all, the emphasis had shifted from "justification by grace" to "justification by works."

The great banner cry of the Reformation and of the groups protesting against Rome was: "bring grace back to the center." Put God's love back to the heart of the Christian faith. Reform the church from a power structure to the fellowship of believers.

What makes us Christian? God's grace. The rest is trappings. But we are eternally tempted to let other things clutter up grace one way or another. Since the "you-get-what-you-deserve" mentality is so much a part of our thinking, we humans tend to let other things intrude into the centrality of grace, and we let those intrusions identify us as Christians, getting in the way of grace.

These become modern forms of the old work righteousness, the things we *do* to make us Christians, or the ways we "legalize" the gospel. We shall see some examples of this in Chapter 8, "Law and Gospel."

It never works. Start tacking additions on to grace, and you are in trouble. Grace stands alone. It must stand alone. All the rest is a result of grace, a response to grace, or a by-product of grace. But salvation is grace, all grace!

In *The Hiding Place* Corrie ten Boom recalls how this truth was impressed on her as a child in Holland. The doctor had informed her family that Aunt Jans had at the most three weeks to live, and Corrie's father broke the news to her.

"My dear sister-in-law," Father began gently, "There is a joyous journey which each of God's children sooner or later sets out on. And, Jans, some must go to their Father empty-handed, but you will run to Him with hands full!"

"All your clubs . . . ," Tante Anna ventured.

"Your writings . . . ," Mama added.

"The funds you've raised . . . ," said Betsie.

"Your talks . . . ," I began.

But our well-meant words were useless. In front of us the proud face crumpled. Tante Jans put her hands over her eyes and began to cry. "Empty, empty!" she choked at last through her tears. "How can we bring anything to God? What does He care for our little tricks and trinkets?"

And then as we listened in disbelief she lowered her hands and with tears still coursing down her face whispered, "Dear Jesus, I thank You that we must come with empty hands. I thank You that You have done all—all—on the Cross, and that all we need in life or death is to be sure of this."

Mama threw her arms around her and they clung together. But I stood rooted to the spot, knowing that I had seen a mystery.

Yes, the mystery she saw was grace. We do not have to count up the clubs we belong to, the talks we give, and the good things we have done in order to know we are safe in God's hand. It is the miracle of grace!

7

How Can I
Receive Grace?

One day I asked my confirmation class, "How would you answer a person who asked you, 'I would really like to have faith in God, but I don't know how'?"

They were puzzled. One girl said, "I would say, 'Just *believe.*' " Another replied, "You pray and read the Bible, and it will come." A boy said, "I don't know, so I would tell that person to go see a pastor. He's supposed to know."

People have asked me that question with urgency and longing in their voices: "How can I believe?"

How does a person become part of this fellowship of grace? If a person has no sense of God in her life, but would like to, what can she do to receive grace? What do we advise people who are wondering, "How do I become a Christian?"

The first step is to give your life to Christ. This act has many names: commitment, surrender, decision, conversion, dedication. Sam Shoemaker, the great

Episcopalian pastor and evangelist, who helped found Alcoholics Anonymous, described this first step:

> Make an act of self-surrender. Do this with another if it will help rivet it, and it very likely will. But make it. Gather up your sins and needs, put them together, bring them to Christ for forgiveness and help. Commit yourself to him in an act of dedication. This act centers in the will, not the emotions. Its reality is not to be determined by whether you see any stars or bright lights, or feel a tingle along your spine; you may and you may not—it is not important. What is important is that you *let go*, let go of your sins and your fears and your inhibitions.

What about those persons who consider themselves Christians or are members of a church, but have never sensed the wonder of grace in their own lives? How many Christians feel they are "missing out on something"? Sam Shoemaker speaks to them too:

> I am shocked to find how many people in our churches have never anywhere made a decisive Christian commitment. They oozed into church membership on a conventional kind of basis, but no one has ever effectively dealt with them spiritually, or helped them make a Christian decision.

In our congregation we have several members who make evangelism calls, talking with people about their faith and spiritual life. We have learned how many people have only the very vaguest idea of what it means to be a Christian. Ask, "Are you a Christian?" and a surprising number of people will answer lamely, "I guess so." With this half-conscious sense of being Christian, they are missing all the joy, strength, meaning, and assurance of being part of God's grace in his church. What is needed here is that step of commitment, a conscious awareness that we are God's.

Surrender is not the last step. It is at the beginning. Christianity cannot be experienced from the outside. You do not grow in the Christian faith by learning a lot *about* it, but by letting the presence of God flood into your life.

This is not something we do for God. We are asking God to do something for us. Our commitment is really calling on him for help: "God, make me yours!" We make our commitment to him, but on second look we realize God enables us to do this by working through his Word and Spirit.

The commitment might be made with faltering steps. A person might be acutely aware of how little he or she knows about the Bible. A person might have many questions about Christian beliefs. But that commitment is the start, like that of the man in the Bible who pleaded to Jesus, "I believe; help my unbelief!" (Mark 9:24).

What happens then? After this surrender, how do we receive grace? How do we grow in grace?

Sometimes when I need sermon ideas I page through the books written by my father, Alvin Rogness. One spring after a tiring Holy Week I was preparing for the Sunday after Easter. The text for that Sunday is the story about Thomas, who could not believe in the resurrection until he saw the risen Lord Jesus for himself, even though the other disciples had described the wonderful experience of seeing him. The point of my father's sermon, "Where Will You Station Yourself?" in *Who Shall Be God?* was that those who are searching for God can "station" themselves at those places where God's grace in Jesus can and will touch them:

> There are three places, where, if you are faithfully stationed, you will have every right to expect the Lord to appear and make his imprint on your life.
> First, in his Word and Sacraments.
> Second, within the fellowship of believers, or his Church.
> Third, in the company of the world's needy.

Needless to say, my sermon that Sunday was heavily "borrowed"!

How can I receive grace? Once we have responded, "Yes, Lord, I want to be yours," we station ourselves where God's grace comes to us. Keep these three stations in mind as we look more closely at this question.

Receiving grace can be a problem for people, because grace is not like a package which can be handed from one to another. Nor is it a set of doctrines or propositions which one can examine, then accept or reject. No, grace is a dynamic, living thing. It is an encounter, a relationship with a person. To receive grace is to experience grace in life, and what we can do is to station ourselves where God's grace is.

How do we do this? Growth in grace takes place in the following ways:

1. *Prayer.* In ways I cannot understand or explain very well, prayer opens the channel between God and me. I do not suppose that I am informing him of anything he does not already know, nor do I think God operates by "majority vote," counting the number of prayers before deciding to do something. But I do know

from my own life and the lives of many others that prayer is vitally important for a living relationship with God.

Many people are skeptical about prayer. Often they become discouraged when they feel their prayers are not answered. I have too. Mark Twain tells how Huckleberry Finn gave up on prayer:

> Then Miss Watson she took me in the closet and prayed, but nothing come of it. She told me to pray every day, and whatever I asked for I would get it. But it warn't so. I tried it. Once I got a fish-line, but no hooks. It warn't any good to me without hooks. I tried for the hooks three or four times, but somehow I couldn't make it work. By and by, one day, I asked Miss Watson to try for me, but she said I was a fool. She never told me why, and I couldn't make it out no way .... No, says I to myself, there ain't nothing in it.

But prayer is not just a shopping list, which we make up once a week as we go to the store.

My experience is that people who become skeptical about prayer are those who do not pray much. If a teenager decides after hearing just a few bars from Beethoven's glorious Ninth Symphony that she does not like it and that classical music is not for her, that would hardly be a fair trial. Nobody will experience the value of prayer without praying. Those who pray regularly discover how much a part of their lives it becomes.

Maybe prayer is like piano playing or skiing. Neither is very rewarding at the beginning. One must spend some time at it before it becomes satisfying.

Many people are far too worried about "how to pray" and "what to say." Prayer is talking to God. When children are secure in their parents' love, they feel free to speak with their parents about anything. They do not have to worry, "What will my parents think if I talk about this or that?" Furthermore, they can ask their parents for anything, even though they know that the parents might not judge it wise to accede to every request.

So it is with God. He is a loving parent, and you can speak with him freely. You will not, after all, be telling him anything he does not already know. Nor do you need to use "religious" language from the King James translation of the Bible. God understands your language just as well.

It is helpful to try to make our prayers more than requests for things. Once a man in our congregation gave us a good guideline for prayer. Remember the word ACTS, he said: "*A*doration, *C*onfession, *T*hanksgiving, and *S*upplication."

> *Adoration*: we tell God in praise how much he means to us.
> *Confession*: we confess what we have done wrong and what bothers us.
> *Thanksgiving*: we thank him for all he has done for us.
> *Supplication*: we come to him with our needs and the needs of others.

It is a good way to realize other elements of prayer besides our requests or supplications.

Much more could be said about prayer, but one thing is certain: in prayer we are drawn closer to God's grace.

2. *Bible study*. The Bible is the record of what God has done for his people throughout the centuries. Chapter 10 will speak more about the Word, so here it is necessary only to stress how indispensable the Bible is for those who wish God to be part of their lives.

There are also dozens of other good Christian books available for study and inspiration. Reading such books puts us into immediate contact with Christians around the world, people who can help us by their experiences, people whom we might otherwise never meet.

3. *The church.* There is no such thing in the Bible as a "lone-wolf" Christian. The Old Testament is about the *people* of Israel, and the New Testament is about the *people* of God in Christ, that is, the Christian church. It would have been inconceivable for somebody to tell the disciples, "I am a follower of Jesus, but I don't want to have anything to do with the church." The incredulous disciples would have answered, "That's impossible! We're in this together!"

Consider all that happens within the church. We worship together. What a thrill it is to join with many others in singing the many glorious hymns we have! We pray together, listen together, and learn together. We are together when a child is baptized. We come forward to receive the body and blood of Christ in Holy Communion together. Within the fellowship of the church we encourage each other and we receive encouragement. We are happy that our children learn about their faith in Sunday school, and we enjoy the elderly whose faith has weathered decades of various experiences and who have become examples for us all. It is within the church that we find opportunities for service, both inside the church as well as through the ways the church reaches out to others.

How much better that is than fooling myself by thinking, "I can do it all alone!"

Have you ever attended a concert, movie, or drama alone and wished you could share the thrill? By being together in the church we share our lives with each other, and all are enriched. We humans are meant to live in community with each other.

A good story from Scotland illustrates this. A man had stopped coming to church. He knew the vicar would soon be calling on him to inquire why. Finally one day the minister did show up at the front door. The man invited him in, and the two sat by the fire. They made small talk, and the man wondered when the discussion would turn to his church attendance.

As the conversation dwindled off, the pastor took the tongs, reached into the fire, took a white-hot coal and set it out in front of the fire. The two taciturn Scots sat there smoking their pipes and sipping their tea. Minutes passed in silence. The coal cooled to red-hot. Slowly the color began to fade. Finally it became black. A wisp of smoke signaled that the fire was out, and the man realized it was an object lesson. "Yes, dominie," he said, "I'll be at the kirk on Sunday."

The coals burned brightly while they were together. When one was removed, it could not long sustain its heat and went out. So we need the fellowship of the church.

4. *Making grace part of our own life.* Station yourself in the company of the world's needy. Grace is not only received; it is lived. We shall see this more clearly in the last chapter. If you wish to know God's grace, be grace-full yourself. That is why grace is a dynamic and living thing. It is the very life of God, and it becomes the basis of our life. We receive grace best when we have reached the point of giving grace through ourselves to those around us.

8

Law and Gospel

Pastors love to talk about "law and gospel," and my impression is that lay people find this twofold emphasis somewhat puzzling.

If you mix law and gospel, you tend to lose grace. We call this tendency "legalism," where the message of the gospel becomes a legal thing, a matter of do's and don'ts. It is probably the most persistent heresy which has plagued the Christian church from its very beginning, and it sneaks up on us in many different ways, as we shall see.

What is the law? What is the gospel? They are different, and if you do not keep them distinct, you will never get Christianity quite right.

One can summarize what the law does in three ways:

1. An awareness of the law is part of God's creation. Every society and every person has a sense of right and wrong. We call it "conscience." (An individual who does not is a "sociopath" or "psychopath," and every society

recognizes this as an aberration or mental illness, something gone wrong.) We might call this characteristic of human beings a part of the "image of God" with which we are created, since God is the source of justice. There is something universal about the Ten Commandments, and every society—Christian or not—recognizes moral standards.

2. When we consider the Ten Commandments and other sayings of God and his prophets in the Bible, we all know that we have fallen short and are imperfect. I have never met anybody who claims to be perfect and without sin. Measured by God's standard, we know that "all have sinned and fall short of the glory of God" (Rom. 3:23). We acknowledge this every time we pray on Sunday morning:

> We confess that we are in bondage to sin and cannot free ourselves. We have sinned against you in thought, word, and deed, by what we have done and by what we have left undone. We have not loved you with our whole heart; we have not loved our neighbors as ourselves (© 1978 *LBW*).

In short, the law condemns us. We realize we cannot be fully righteous before God on the basis of our fulfilling the law.

3. The law also shows us Christians how to live. This is law in a quite different sense, because once we are saved the law no longer condemns. It is not the law in the sense of legal requirements, but it is a guide for our willing response to the love that has been given us. So one must be careful not to make this "third use" of the law a legalistic thing.

Each of these three uses of the law is distinctive, and we must take care how we use the word *law*.

In one sense the law is wonderful, yes, even joyful and delightful. The psalmist wrote that the godly man's "delight is in the law of the Lord, and on this law he meditates both day and night" (Ps. 1:2). The longest chapter in the entire Bible is an exultant praise of God's law:

> Oh, how I love thy law!...
> I love thy commandments above gold...
> Thy testimonies are wonderful...
> With open mouth I pant,
> because I long for thy commandments.
>   Ps. 119:97, 127, 129, 131

Here we are dealing with the first and third uses of the law: God was gracious enough to create us with the capacity for right and wrong, and he gave us in clear words the gifts of the Ten Commandments, the command to love, and his other commands, so that we might know the way to happiness in his will. The law is our road map to bountiful living. Thanks be to God for that! In this sense the law is "good news."

But when we contrast law and gospel, as we shall do in this chapter, we think of the law in its accusing function. This second use of the law reminds me that if I were to be judged by the law, I would be condemned.

You may have learned this little saying in Sunday school: "The law shows us our need of a Savior. The gospel shows us the Savior we need." This is the second use of the law: to accuse us and lead us to Christ. When we contrast law and gospel, it is this second use of the law that we have in mind.

Any time you read a Bible verse and realize your shortcomings, that is the law at work. Any time you read a Bible verse and realize what God has done for your salvation, that is the gospel at work.

Can anybody read, "You shall not covet," and not feel a stab of guilt? We all covet. Can anybody read, "Love your enemy and pray for him who persecutes you," and not realize we fall short? That is the law. It accuses us and points to our shortcomings.

On the other hand, what is your reaction when you hear Jesus' words, "I am the bread of life," "I am the good shepherd," or, "Come to me, all who labor and are heavy laden, and I will give you rest"? You cannot help but feel the warmth of God's hand around you. Can anybody help but feel wonderful in reading Paul's words that nothing "will be able to separate us from the love of God in Christ Jesus our Lord" (Rom. 8:39)? Those are words of gospel, words of pure grace.

Strangely enough, the same words might be both law and gospel. When Jesus said, "Follow me," to Matthew and "Hurry down out of that tree, Zacchaeus, for I'm eating at your house today," each of those devious tax collectors felt both law and gospel. The invitation was law, because it made them acutely aware that they were sinners. But those invitations were gospel too, because they caused those two hearts to leap for joy. Those two crooks could not help but wonder that this marvelous man wanted to be with them!

The Bible is full of law and gospel, and we need to hear them both. But we must keep them straight. Mix one into the other, and you are in trouble.

The trouble comes when we "legalize" the gospel, or make it into law. Rather than a joyous relationship of faith in the triune God, Christianity then becomes a grim set of rules and regulations. Grace is squished out, and law replaces gospel.

It happens all the time.

I ask my confirmation class each year to finish the sentence, "A Christian is one who . . . ." Some answers are, ". . . one who does the Ten Commandments, goes to church on Sunday, reads the Bible". . . . "one who tries to do God's will". . . . "one who goes to church and does good things," etc. I am not against any of these items mentioned, but the answers have legalized Christianity by defining it with laws and works. These works are meant to be consequences of the Christian faith. In defining a Christian, faith in Father, Son, and Holy Spirit must be the central definition. The others follow.

In Chapter 2 I mentioned the well-intentioned but revealing comments one hears at funerals. I stand next to the coffin of a lady who is surely one of God's great saints. Somebody says, "If anybody is in heaven, she is. She was always kind and never said a mean word about anybody." The words are meant well and are true, but the emphasis is misplaced. I too believe that person is in heaven, but it is because she trusted in the wonder of God's grace in Christ. The rest followed after.

It is a terrible thing to make the gospel into law, because then we are bound to start comparing how we do in comparison with others. We fall into the quicksand of the Pharisees, where how well one did was the test of faith, rather than resting back in the hand of God secure in his grace. If we make the gospel into law, then we are never secure, but always have to worry whether or not we have done enough.

There are several modern versions of this "work righteousness," in which our identity as Christians is measured by our performance rather than by grace.

1. *Doctrine.* There are people who think they are true Christians because they believe the right things. Other denominations are not only different, they believe, but they are just plain wrong, and therefore one should avoid contact with Christians from other churches. One should not even pray with them, to say nothing of communing with them or listening to them.

There are historical reasons for the existence of various denominations. Some of these reasons still exist, and others fade with time, but the fact that towers over all these differences is that we are all children under God's goodness and grace. Our differences pale beside this great affirmation, and we should never let our differences in doctrine—as crucial as we think they are—obscure the unity we have in that wonderful truth.

2. *Experience and feelings.* "Born again" is an important word for Christians. Most major denominations define "born again" as that which happens at Baptism. Religious experiences after Baptism can be profoundly moving and be a decisive part of one's life, but one has been "born again" in Baptism. Others identify being "born again" as an emotional or religious experience when one becomes aware of Jesus' presence or work, or when one consciously commits one's life to Jesus. For them the important thing is that one can point to the beginning of a "personal" relationship with Jesus.

Such feelings, emotions and experiences are necessary and good for Christian growth, but they do not define my being as a Christian. When "born-again" persons describe their experiences, I am grateful on their behalf. But if such persons look askance at me because I did not have the same experience, then I realize that they are defining Christianity as those experiences and insisting that I should have the same. God's grace works with me in a different way than he works with you. Our unity is that we are both children of grace, not that our experiences and feelings are identical to each other.

3. *Being "religious."* Such things as prayer, worship, singing hymns, etc., are part of strengthening faith, but "being religious" is not the identity of being a Christian. Some have the idea that to be a true Christian one should not have a part of the affairs of this world. The truth is that a Christian can and should live this life with gusto, fully a part of his society, neighborhood, profession, family, and other human concerns. It is difficult to criticize anybody for being "too religious," but it is grace that makes a Christian, not being religious. The sentence, "Those persons cannot be Christians because they are not religious enough," makes no sense. Such persons might be neglecting the opportunities to strengthen faith, but one cannot conclude they are therefore not Christian.

4. *Church activity.* We are active in our congregations because we have discovered there worthwhile opportunities both for enriching our personal and family life as well as for service to God. But it is incorrect to conclude that others who are not as active are not "as Christian" as we. We are saved and made Christian by grace, not by church participation, as important as such participation is to us and to our church. (The other side of the coin is that those who think they can be Christian

on their own, without the fellowship and communion with other believers in a local congregation, have not read their Bibles correctly.)

5. *Political position.* It has become popular to conclude that persons are not Christian if they have certain positions on political issues. Christians on the right condemn as un-Christian those who disagree with them on abortion and homosexuality. Christians on the left condemn as un-Christian those who disagree with them on disarmament and ecology. I once heard a Christian leader say on television that a prominent Christian political leader could not be a reborn Christian because he voted a certain way!

This is a sensitive issue, because the Christian faith is deeply involved and concerned with many moral issues in politics. We feel strongly about them, for sincere and intelligent Christians do disagree. But since it is grace that makes us one, we need to learn that political positions neither identify us as Christians, nor should such disagreements divide us as brothers and sisters in Christ.

All these five items listed above are good things, in their proper context. But when they get in the way of the gospel of grace—as they so often seem to do—then they can warp our whole understanding of what a Christian is. We cannot move the law into the realm of gospel and legalize the Christian faith.

But mixing the law and gospel in the other direction—moving the gospel into the realm of law and eliminating the law—is equally troublesome.

It is popular today to think, "God is such a friendly fellow, so if we are decent and responsible citizens, we shall somehow muddle our way to heaven." We patronize God by calling him "the man upstairs" or "my buddy God," or some other trivial term. A good many Americans believe in a "great Mush-God," as someone wrote, a blurred sort of divine being who is always congenial and does not get too upset by human vagrancies. If we are moderately good, he will welcome us into heaven like a celestial Rotary Club president shaking hands with upstanding citizens. This view does not understand grace, because it does not need grace. Such wooly-headed thinking, though widespread, ignores both Old and New Testaments.

No, God is the awesome, majestic creator of this whole universe. He is a God whose love of justice caused Mount Sinai to rumble and shake, a God who has created us with a capacity for justice and order, and has laid down for us the standards by which human society will work.

God did not give us the law to spoil our fun. He gave us the Ten Commandments to inform us how human life is lived at its best. When we disobey, we mess things up for ourselves and those around us. You can no more disobey God's law without consequences than you can disregard the law of gravity, jump off a 10-story building, and hope for no consequences!

God cares a great deal how we live. He is both saddened and angered when he sees the regularity with which we humans make each other miserable and suffer. God created us in his own image and breathed into us the breath of life. He must be appalled when he watches what we do to each other on this earth of his! To say, "He realizes we aren't doing very well, but—

good fellow that he is—he'll shrug it off," is a superficial mockery of all that God is.

To dissolve the law into a pseudo-gospel cheapens the real gospel. If God is so casual about our sins and will wave them off with a shrug of his shoulders, why did Jesus come to earth and die? Ernest Campbell made a biting comment on this "Mush-God" of our century by suggesting that in addition to the "seven words" from the cross Jesus may well have uttered an eighth: "If I'm OK and you're OK, what am I doing here?"

The grandeur of the cross is that this great and just God who judges sin could not bear to condemn these human beings, whom he created and whom he loves. So he sent his Son, who suffered the consequence and punishment of evil on our part, then was raised to life in victory. He took our place in suffering that we might receive his place with God. He gave himself for us, so that we could be held in the hand of God—the story of grace.

One of the best phrases Martin Luther used was in Latin—*simul justus et peccator*, "simultaneously just and sinner." It describes us. We are just in the eyes of God by his grace in Jesus Christ. We have been justified. But we are still sinners. We expect improvement in our lives as God's Spirit takes hold in our hearts, and we try to follow his will, but the taint of sin will never disappear. There are no "perfect Christians," even though sometimes we expect others to be that.

The reason this Latin phrase is so good is that it reminds us that we always need Jesus. We need always to be aware of that second use of the law—to show us our need of a Savior. If we would become perfect at the moment of conversion, then we would be proud of our perfection and not need Jesus anymore. But there is no room for pride before God. It is all a story of his grace. I need not grovel in despair over my remaining sins, for I am held in God's constant forgiveness. But I do need to recall daily that I stand repentant in need of Christ's righteousness and pray that the Holy Spirit will work within me to battle that sin which still lurks.

Martin Luther began the explanation of each of the Ten Commandments with the same two words: "We are to *fear and love* God so that . . . ." God is not a bumbling old man with a long beard and white choir robe sitting on a cloud, as cartoonists portray. The *fear* we have standing before him is the awe we have at being in the presence of the Creator and Master of the universe, the God of righteousness and justice.

The most famous sermon ever preached in colonial America was Jonathan Edwards' "Sinners in the Hands of an Angry God." If all we saw in God was law and anger, how could we possibly love him? We could not. But there is also the gospel, the good news that this God loves us. We are also "sinners in the hands of a loving Father," and because he has so loved us, we love him in response.

The best way I know of understanding this dual nature of God is to look at parents. Parents love their children, but they also lay down laws, *for the good of the children.* Every wise and good parent knows there must be laws and discipline. Letting a child grow up without discipline is a sign not of love but of neglect. I know from experience how difficult it is to go past the supermarket candy counter with a pleading and crying child, but I do so out of love. A child might know her parents love her, but impending discipline may also generate awe and fear in the child's heart!

There are times in our lives when we feel God more as a God of law than of gospel. Every single one of us has looked heavenward with a cry of "Why?" "Why did this happen?" is an anguished question which we ask, sometimes with tearful eye, other times with clenched fist, perhaps with both. The world is full of events that make us wonder how God can be a God of grace and gospel.

Sometimes such events make us ask, "Can God be so insensitive, uncaring, unloving?"

I have known people who have quite literally "given up" on God. They have looked about in the world, or suffered a calamity in their lives, and they have concluded that if such things happen, there cannot be a God of love.

There is no pat answer to this agony. When I stood at the bedside with parents watching their 10-year-old girl and only child die of cancer, I raged inside at the cruelty of this universe which allows such things to happen. I too wanted to ask God, "Why?"

I know this is a sinful world and that war, accidents, disease, starvation, and other scourges of mankind are among us. I also know that we humans bring much of it upon ourselves. But I plead with God to intervene and prevent some of it, and of course being human I ask him to act in those instances in which I am involved.

My own life was free of major tragedy until I lost my brother when I was 25 and he had just turned 24. I was closer to him than to anybody else. He was killed by a truck which he did not see coming. Why did God let that happen? I was angry at God, for the first time in my life. But I made a discovery: in my grief and anger, I had no place else to turn but to God. I was mad at God, but where else could I turn? I believe that at the moment my brother's heart stopped beating God reached down and took him in his arms. Whatever sense would it have made for me to cut myself off in anger from the One who was holding my brother in his care right then and who stood ready to help me through this too?

Furthermore, I am certain that God was neither surprised nor irritated by my anger, and being a gracious Father he surely did not love me less during that time.

Certainly there are occasions in your own life when you have felt a God of law facing you. Maybe tragedy has struck, or suffering, or sickness, or death of a loved one, and you are tempted to reject God as unloving or unlistening. Or you have done something you know is wrong, and the thought of God causes you to tremble in fear or guilt. Maybe you would have preferred to hide from God, like Adam and Eve after sinning (Gen. 3:8).

So you know him as a God of law. Tell him! Tell him your fear. Tell him your guilt. Tell him your anger. You can, because he is also the God of the gospel. So tell him. Do not just leave him.

Remember you are speaking to a God who knows the suffering you are experiencing. He suffered the agonies of rejection, loneliness, pain, and death through his Son. Undoubtedly the suffering and hardships in this world continue to pain him, for that is not what he created. The question of evil and suffering are too complex for us here, but we are assured that we can always go to a loving God who has experienced the worst this world can inflict. He understands, and we can turn to him.

Martin Luther was fond of speaking of the "left" and "right" hand of God. The left hand is his work through law. It is the side of God we are afraid of, the God of justice and anger, from whom we shrink in guilt and fear. God's right hand is his reaching out with the gospel. It is his love and grace, which reaches into the tragedies and hardships of human life with a healing, comforting, and strengthening hand.

Luther called the left hand of God the "hidden God." We cannot learn to know him fully through the law. If we see only that side of him, his true nature is hidden from us.

But the right hand of God is the "revealed God." It is through the gospel we know him as he really is. Through the gospel we learn to know and experience his grace.

9

The Means of Grace

Every summer we spend a week at Camp Vermilion with our confirmation students. One summer I asked them, "Do any of you know what the term, 'the means of grace,' is about?" Nobody did. That did not surprise me.

So I rephrased the question, "What are the means, or ways, that God's grace comes to us?" Blank faces.

I made another run at it: "How do we find out that God loves us?"

An answer came: "The Bible." Good, now we are getting warm.

"Any other ways?"

Another answer: "We go to church."

"And what happens at church to show us God's love?"

"We listen to the Bible." "We listen to the sermon." "We sing hymns about God." "We pray."

"And what happens when we bring little children forward, and when we come forward ourselves to the altar toward the end of a service?"

"Baptism, Lord's Supper—yes, the sacraments."

They knew the answers, but the term "means of grace" was strange to them.

So I told them, "If you forget everything else we learn this week at camp, try to remember this: 'The *means of grace*, that is, the ways by which God's grace and love comes to us, are *the Word and the sacraments.*'"

During the following year in our classes I repeated that line a few times. At the close of our study, during the month before the service of confirmation, I have each student come in for an "interview," when we talk about the meaning of confirmation. During these interviews last year I asked the same question, "What are the means of grace?"

One said, "Jesus and the Bible." Another said, "Baptism, the church." Others said, "Praying, Communion, Sunday school, other people," and so on. Not one student answered clearly and simply, "the Word and the sacraments."

It all goes to show, I think, that *grace* and *means of grace* are technical terms pastors use, but are not part of anybody else's vocabulary. These are good students, and their answers are good. God's grace does come through these items they named, plus others. My confirmation class may have difficulty remembering that "the means of grace are the Word and sacraments" because their good instincts tell them that one can never limit God's grace. True, grace is conveyed specifically by Word and sacrament, but in the end, does it not just spill out all over God's universe?

I am touched by God's grace when I stand on the shore of a northern lake and watch the rays of the setting sun set the clouds ablaze with splashes of red and yellow.

I am touched by God's grace when I stand with a young couple at the window of the hospital nursery and see the look on their faces when they point to their newborn baby.

I am touched by God's grace when I sit at the bedside of an aged saint in his last hour of life with his hand in mine and he whispers to me, "I am ready to meet God."

I am touched by God's grace when I visit a person recently home from the hospital, and somebody from our church rings the doorbell to bring a hot dish for the family, and I notice a few other dishes in the refrigerator, also recently arrived.

I am touched by God's grace when a bride gets choked up as she says her wedding vows to the young man at her side.

I am touched by God's grace when my older children ask me for some advice, or when my littlest one crawls over to my lap when the bad guys in *Superman II* scare him.

I am touched by God's grace when a brash junior-high school boy called me, "Hey, preach!" (his mother gasped), and we both knew it was a sign of affection and that he will always remember the day he looked me in the eye at his confirmation service and said, "Yes, by the help of God."

Grace is all over the place. Just look for it, and you cannot miss it. It surprises you in hospital rooms, jail cells, football fields, battlefields, and in many other places, even where there is wickedness, sickness, cruelty, brutality, and death. Even where people do not recognize it and name it, there it is—the gift of grace. It is there moving among people who do not know the name of God or who call him by names which are strange to our ears. Some people in Russia, Albania, or China, may try their best to slam the door on God's existence, but the hand of God moves in and among them too.

An old Jewish story tells of the smart skeptic who once sneered at a famous rabbi, Yitzak Meir, "I'll give you a gulden if you can show me where God lives!" The wise rabbi answered, "And I'll give you two gulden if you can show me where he doesn't!"

God's grace is wherever he is, and that wonderful Psalm 139 tells us that he is always with us:

> You are all around me on every side;
> you protect me with your power . . . .
> Where could I go to escape from you?
> Where could I get away from your presence?
> If I went up to heaven, you would be there;
> if I lay down in the world of the dead, you would be there.
> If I flew away beyond the east
> or lived in farthest place in the west,
> you would be there to lead me,
> you would be there to help me.
> I could ask the darkness to hide me
> or the light around me to turn into night,
> but even darkness is not dark for you,
> and the night is as bright as the day (Ps. 139:5-12 TEV).

Yet even though God is everywhere, we do not always see his grace or recognize when we are touched by it.

Sometimes we might think it is difficult to see the hand of God. At times it is.

But God does not play peekaboo with us. He reveals himself to us—concretely and tangibly—and that is the importance of the Word and sacraments as means of grace. We may or may not recognize God's grace through the beauty of nature or the love of other people, but he reveals himself and comes to us in direct ways through these means of grace. Without them, we would search and grope for signs of God's presence. But God uses the Word and the sacraments as means by which he comes to us in unmistakably plain and clear ways. When we understand the Word and sacraments as means of grace, we are able to grasp their purpose. What are they for? To convey to us God's grace in a specific and special way. Once we receive his grace through them, then we can begin to see it in all those other places as well.

10

The Word of God

The Word is a *huge* word! We use it in four ways: (1) God speaking, (2) Jesus, (3) the Bible, and (4) the words about God spoken or written by others.

Look at the first verses of John's gospel:

> In the beginning was the Word, and the Word was with God, and the Word was God. He was in the beginning with God; all things were made through him, and without him was not anything made that was made .... And the Word became flesh and dwelt among us, full of grace and truth; we have beheld his glory, glory as of the only Son from the Father (John 1:1-14).

The Greek term John used for "Word" was *logos*, which means much more than our English "word." The *logos* is what one thinks, or intends—what one *is*, really—which is then expressed outwardly. Words are our most direct means of expressing our thoughts and intentions, so *logos* is most often translated "word."

John's gospel reminds us how God created the world: he *spoke*, and his Word brought creation into being.

God's Word is the outward expression of *what he is*. In the Old Testament we read of God speaking to people, or speaking to people indirectly through other people, such as the prophets. But in the New Testament God's Word took on a new form in coming to human beings: "And the Word became flesh and dwelt among us."

Jesus is the most tangible, concrete and visible expression—or revelation—of God. Everything God is was brought to life in this person Jesus, his Son who lived among us on earth.

Jesus was God's Word. Everything he did and said on this earth was God's Word in human form.

Who is God, and what is he or she like? What more profound question is there among human beings?

The disciple Philip was much like one of us, and he wondered the same thing. During that tense and anxious evening before Jesus was crucified, just a few minutes after Jesus and his men had finished the Last Supper, even as the religious authorities were preparing to arrest him, Jesus said to his disciples, "If you had known me, you would have known my Father also; henceforth you know him and have seen him" (John 14:7). That sounded like double talk to Philip, so he just blurted out what most of us would have wondered too: "Lord, show us the Father, and we shall be satisfied."

Jesus turned to him and replied with that momentous answer, "Have I been with you so long, and yet you do not know me, Philip? He who has seen me has seen the Father" (John 14:9).

There it is, the big answer! You want to know who God is? Look to Jesus. He is the "Word made flesh."

God had told about himself in the Old Testament, both directly and through the prophets. He could have done it in even grander style, with an overpowering celestial loud-speaking system broadcasting his voice in all languages simultaneously from the heavens so that nobody would miss the point. But we would still wonder what *we* should be like, how those loud-speaker instructions ought to be translated into living.

But in Jesus God came directly to life on earth, right down to our level, so there could be no mistaking what he was like in the context of human life.

All those other fleeting glimpses of God and his grace that illumine our lives—the beautiful sunsets, the moments of love between people, the joys of life—might be vague and puzzling, or even unrecognizable, if it were not for the fact that God has stared us full in the face as a human being in Jesus.

My first real acquaintance with classical music was Beethoven's *Fifth* and Schubert's *Unfinished*, the two sides of the introductory record I received when I joined a record club for the first time. I played that record until the grooves almost wore out. Before that, I would not have recognized the pieces by hearing only a few measures. Nor would I have recognized it if just one instrument played its part of the music. But once I learned to know those symphonies, hearing only several measures, or hearing one part, or even whistling one of the melodies evoked the beauty of the music in my mind. Any part of it reminded me of the glorious whole.

That is how it is knowing Jesus. Little signs of God's grace here and there are obscure. But when one knows how God brought goodness and beauty into human life through Jesus, the goodness and the beauty one sees in the world are immediately apparent as a sign of God's hand reaching down.

News of Jesus might not have reached us through all these centuries if somebody had not written the story down shortly after it all happened. Or, as you know from your own experience in passing on stories, the news about Jesus would have become totally unreliable. But fortunately for us some persons who were right there on the scene and others who talked with eyewitnesses wrote it down for us.

That, in short, is why the Bible is so precious to us. It is God's Word because it brings us God's Word. It is not grace itself, but it is a *means* of grace, a means by which God's grace comes to us.

What a monstrous tragedy it is that the Bible has become a battleground among Christians! Rather than revel joyously over what the Bible brings us, too many Christians wrangle with those who do not agree with their own interpretations. Words such as *inerrant* and *infallible*, which are not even in the Bible, are hurled back and forth as artillery by Christians who think they are protecting the Bible and behave in a grotesquely un-Christian manner in doing so.

Paul tells us, "All Scripture is inspired by God and profitable for teaching, for reproof, for correction, and for training in righteousness" (2 Tim. 3:16. For Paul "Scripture" is of course the Old Testament.) But the Bible does not go into any detail about itself. Surely we can agree that God's Spirit did whatever was necessary to move the biblical authors to write their books, and he saw to it that enough information was included in these books so that we can know what is sufficient.

The whole point is that the Bible is an immeasurably cherished book for us. How many times have I watched the power of those words flow almost visibly to people when I have read to them: "The Lord is my shepherd, I shall not want" (Ps. 23:1). Or, "I lift up my eyes to the hills. From whence does my help come? My help comes from the Lord, who made heaven and earth" (Ps. 121:1-2). There is strength there, strength most of us hardly even tap.

Listen to people who have had everything taken away from them, all their props kicked out from under them. They have turned to the old familiar words of the Bible. Listen to those Americans who were held hostage in Iran for 444 days. Many of them went back to the Bible, dredging up from their memories every verse they could remember and savoring them day after day. Thomas E. Schaefer, the highest-ranking military officer in the embassy when it was overrun on November 5, 1979, read his Bible several times through during that fearful time of captivity. During one two-week period he was put into solitary confinement without his Bible and was forced to rely on his memory. He recalls:

> Several times I just got down on my knees and said, "God, I cannot handle this. I need your help." And I got it.

Kathryn Koob, another hostage, wrote that on the day after their capture

I reached back into my mind to see what I could find. Were the hymns, the psalms, and Bible verses there? Yes! Their words filled my mind ... a vast treasure of worship and devotional materials from my earliest childhood days .... And I thank God for my parents, who insisted that we know our Bible verses.

She remembers Christmas 1979, when she finally received a Bible in her captivity: "It was almost too much. I could scarcely do anything but sit and hold that precious volume."

Sometime when you are with friends, pose this question: "If you were stuck on a desert island for a long time and could have only three books with you, which would you choose?" Most would include a Bible. Yet how many of us have spent much time in the last month reading it? We agree it is a precious book, but it may be one of the most neglected precious books on our shelves.

The Word as a means of grace is God's words, Jesus, the Bible, and also those words we speak and write about God. Whenever we tell the story—from the pulpit, in Sunday school, in hospitals, in living rooms, or on the street—those words are conveying God. Our words are in a different category from Jesus and the Bible, but the Word is there.

The most foolish of all proverbs in the English language is "Sticks and stones may break my bones, but words will never hurt me." Parents like that saying, to let their children know they should not be bothered when others tease them. But it is not true.

The reverse is the case: nothing hurts as much as words can. The saying should really go: "Sticks and stones just break my bones, but words can really hurt me!" Words are the most powerful things in the whole world, for good and for bad. Words can make or break a human being. There is nothing as wonderful as hearing, "I love you," and nothing hurts more than, "I don't like you anymore."

Imagine the suspense at the end of a jury trial when the defendant waits to hear those brief words from the foreman of the jury. How much hangs on whether those words will be "Guilty" or "Not guilty."

The Bible knows the power of words. It all started in Genesis, when God spoke those booming words, "Let there be light," and the universe was on its way, word-by-word, day-by-day, through creation. (If you doubt the power and effect of words, look up some or all of these: 2 Sam. 12:1-14; 18:31-33; Mark 4:39-41; Luke 4:31-37; 5:17-28; 7:6-10; John 4:46-53; Acts 7:51-60).

When Jesus was sleeping in a boat as a storm threatened to capsize the craft, the terrified disciples woke him. Jesus sat up, probably grabbed the gunwale for support, and with the wind whipping his hair all over his face, he spoke—just words. "Peace! Be still!" And the storm calmed. What power! (Mark 4:37-41).

A Roman centurion's favorite servant was dying, and the officer sent to Jesus for help. Jesus set off, but the soldier sent a messenger to tell Jesus it was not necessary for him to come all that way. "I am a man who lives by command," was his message to Jesus, "When I say, 'Go,' 'Come,' or 'Do this,' the words are obeyed. Only say the word and my servant will be healed." Jesus was astonished to hear somebody perceive the power of his word. Jesus spoke, and the servant was healed (Matt. 8:5-13 paraphrase).

Jesus was speaking in a crowded house, and a paralyzed man's friends opened the skylight to lower the man down. "Your sins are forgiven," Jesus told the man, words which made the authorities angry at Jesus for speaking words of forgiveness. Then Jesus spoke again, "Rise, take up your pallet and go home." Much to his own surprise, the man could move those stiffened legs, and he arose and walked through the crowd, which was hushed in awe (Mark 2:1-12).

The Bible is full of powerful words like those. Again and again, what was the reaction of the crowd to Jesus?

They were all amazed and said to one another, "What is this word? For with authority and power he commands the unclean spirits, and they come out" (Luke 4:36).

The gospel message which we bring is a story, told with words. It is an incredible story about a love so strong that it died to bring us life. We come to the world with this story, and we tell it with simple everyday words. But in those words there is the Word, and that Word is a means through which flows the grace of God.

11

The Sacraments

The Christian outlook went awry a few decades after Jesus, when people began thinking that the soul and spirit were good, but the body was bad. This notion has cropped up again and again all through the church's history and has caused no end of mischief.

In the Middle Ages it caused devout Christians to forsake the affairs of the world and close themselves up into monasteries and convents, believing that a real Christian is one who is removed from the world and devotes one's time more exclusively to "spiritual" pursuits, such as prayer and meditation. "Get away from the world," was their motto.

During the time of the Reformation this impulse produced much destruction of church art. Some people believed that to be really Christian one had to remove worldly art from church buildings, so stained glass windows were smashed, statues were thrown into rivers, pictures of biblical persons and scenes were destroyed

or covered over, and church interiors were white-
washed—all in the name of "true religion."

We see this same kind of outlook around us today.
A young man told me he was not going to college because the only thing worth studying was the Bible. He
disdained all earthly culture, learning, and beauty as
un-Christian, as if God did not want us to be involved
in this world at all. I recall as a student hearing a speaker urge us to participate as Christians in the human
affairs of the world. A man questioned him afterward
by saying, "You must have trouble with 1 John 2:15, 'Do
not love the world or the things in the world.'" (And
of course when the word "world" refers to the sinful
order apart from God's kingdom, then we are indeed
not a part of it.) To which the speaker replied, "Yes, I
admit I am uneasy with that wording and how it is so
often misunderstood. But then," he smiled at the ques-
tioner, "I suppose you have trouble with John 3:16, 'For
God so loved the world...'!"

The fact is that Christianity is the most "worldly" of
all of the world's religions. The world is not something
opposite of God, to be escaped from (as it is in so many
religions). It is God's good creation.

Look at Jesus. He was a man vitally concerned about
this world. People hungry? He did not say, "Food is not
important. Just think about spiritual things." No, he fed
them. People sick? He did not say, "Forget the pain and
read the Scriptures instead." No, he healed them. He
enjoyed the revelry of a wedding celebration, even fur-
nishing more wine for it.

Look again at Jesus. Was he a spiritual, ghostly ap-
parition? No, he was a human being, as much a part of
this physical world as you and I. He was born in a barn.

He had to be diapered and burped. No doubt he woke weary Joseph and Mary up at inconvenient times by crying and fussing. Like other growing children he probably complained abut eating vegetables. Oh yes, he was a very, very special human being, but he was *fully* a human being! He was "God's Word," but he was also "made flesh," as John wrote.

God intends not that we should abandon the world to become holy, but that we should become holy and restore this world to its Creator.

What does all this have to do with sacraments? In the sacraments God is using something *worldly* to come to us. He uses things touchable, concrete, tastable, and visible to convey his grace to us.

What did he use as a sign for making us a part of his people? Water, the water of Baptism. The symbolism of water is clear enough. First, water is most commonly used for washing, just as returning to God is to be washed and forgiven. Second, water is used for drinking, so necessary for life that we would not survive a week without water. So is God necessary for true living. Third, notice the ordinariness of water. God did not use fine wine, or even orange juice. He used the most common thing in all the earth, which can be found wherever there are people, even in desert oases. It is a reminder that God is everywhere, not just in hidden, out-of-the-way places. Water is the perfect sign to convey all aspects of Baptism.

What did he use for conveying to us his special presence? What would be more appropriate than a special, extra fancy gourmet food, since Jesus was such a special person. No, he chose bread and wine. They were just the plain bread and table wine that the poorest household would be using at any ordinary meal. He did not even use good bread, but the flat, cracker-like unyeasted bread of the Passover meal. It was the most ordinary and available food found in any home. (Unfortunately, this symbolism is not as obvious to us, since most of us do not drink wine at every meal, and the more convenient wafers are usually used rather than ordinary bread.)

What is a sacrament? When the New Testament was translated into Latin, the original Greek word *mysterion* was translated with two Latin words, sometimes *mysterium* and other times *sacramentum*. For instance, Colossians 1:27 reads in Latin, ". . . this *sacramentum*, which is Christ in you, the hope of glory." Ephesians 5:32 in Latin is, "This is a great *sacramentum*, and I take it to mean Christ and the church." Our English versions now use only "mystery," so the word "sacrament" is not in our Bibles anymore.

Since the Latin Bible was universally used in the western half of the Christian church for over 1000 years, it is no wonder that it heavily influenced the vocabulary of the church. Substitute the word "sacrament" for "mystery" in the following verses where it occurs in the Latin, and you can sense how the word came to be understood: Eph. 1:9; 3:3,9; 5:32; Col. 1:27; 1 Tim. 3:16, and Rev. 1:20; 10:7; 17:7. In other cases Greek, Latin, and English all use *mysterion/mysterium*/mystery. (See Rom. 11:25; 16:25; 1 Cor. 15:51; Eph. 3:4; 6:19; Col. 1:26; 2:2; 4:3; 2 Thess. 2:7; 1 Tim. 3:9; Rev. 17:5.)

The real mystery/*sacramentum* is Jesus, God's salvation for us. What we now call sacraments—Baptism and Communion—are those gifts God has granted us as part of his plan, ways that Jesus employs to draw us closer to him—means of grace.

Since the number of sacraments is not made clear in the Bible, your count will depend on your definition. I understand a sacrament to be:

1. a rite given and commanded by Christ for all believers,
2. using visible means,
3. to convey grace (and all the benefits of grace, such as forgiveness, etc.).

All Christians recognize Baptism and Communion as sacraments. Whether one considers other church rites as sacraments depends on one's definition.

The sacraments represent and embody in an earthly way what grace is.

Grace is a gift of God, which we cannot deserve or qualify for. Who could deserve less or qualify less for something than a little baby? There is *nothing* that baby has done. Grace can only be a gift. In the Baptism of an infant, God is saying, "This child has done nothing yet, but I want her as a child of mine and part of my family on earth." The child is embraced by God and by the church from that moment on. Everything the gospel offers belongs now to that child—forgiveness, the presence of the Spirit, fellowship in the church, and so on. Just as Baptism is a sign of God's acceptance and washing, so the promises the parents and godparents make are signs of the grace that infant will receive through the church. The dynamics of the Christian faith and life—grace received and then passed on to others—are present as that child is baptized.

The reason some churches do not baptize infants is that they understand Baptism differently. For them it is a statement of faith, so naturally they wait until a teenager or adult can make such a statement. We believe that in the New Testament Baptism is becoming part of God's family, the church. Then infants of believing parents can and should be part of the church too, just as in the New Testament whole households were baptized with the parents.

Holy Communion is clearly Jesus' way of giving us a concrete means of his presence. We know, of course, that "where two or three are gathered together in my name, there am I in the midst of them" (Matt. 18:20). But the Lord's Supper is unique. There he comes to us through something visible and concrete—bread and wine. We believe that Communion is more than just a reminder, sign, or symbol of Jesus' presence. We believe he meant what he said: "This is my body .... This is my blood." In a mysterious yet physical way he is indeed "truly present" in the bread and wine, even though the bread and wine remain bread and wine.

The whole point of the sacraments is that God's grace comes to us through ordinary, worldly means. Grace is not esoteric, found only in fancy places or in intricate rituals. It comes right into the common arena of human life, as available as water, bread, and wine.

Does this commonness detract from the wonder of grace? Not at all. Rather, it exalts the glory of God's created world. The most ordinary can convey God's grace—water, bread, wine, and yes, a baby in a smelly Bethlehem barn!

For some people the most sublime moment of Christian worship is the thrilling sound of a great organ and choir in a massive cathedral. For others of a mystical nature the peak of Christian worship might come during those moments when they become lost in wonder during their own meditation and contemplation. Others look for an inspiring sermon.

These can be wonderful moments, but they are not where God chose to make his grandest entry into life and worship. There are relatively few great cathedrals with huge organs and choirs. Just a few of us are mystics. Not everybody is equally moved by sermons. No, God does not enter the stage just at those times. While our eyes might be focused on those mountain-top experiences, he enters very simply, with water, bread, and wine—the most ordinary means he could find. That is where his grace comes flooding into our lives.

Those other moments are inspiring and moving, but the really unsurpassable drama in Christian worship—when, I like to think, even the angels pause from their activities and look downward—is when a child is brought forward to have some water sprinkled on, or when people come forward for a piece of bread and sip of wine. *That* is drama! At those moments we are not spectators, watching from the sidelines. We are there, drawn into that great action.

Has it ever struck you that the sacraments seem the *least solemn* moments of worship? Not only do they use such everyday items as water, bread, and wine, but the very settings of the sacraments prevent them from being overly dignified or even outwardly very impressive. What is going on in the sacraments is awesome, even though both the means and actions are very commonplace—just the way they were intended to be.

There is something so wonderfully human and ordinary about the sacraments! A family around the baptismal font might try to be as solemn as possible, but the human touch always creeps in. One of the older children starts whispering during the prayer, or turns around and waves at somebody in the congregation, or sticks her finger in the water to check the temperature, or starts exploring around the chancel. Just at the moment of Baptism Uncle Albert breaks the spell by slipping his Instamatic out of his pocket and popping a flash picture. And often the mother's worst fears are realized when the baby, who *always* sleeps during this time and was awakened extra early this morning to guarantee exhaustion during the service, cries through half the Baptism!

Communion is the same. You find your mind wandering all over while waiting in line. At the altar rail you pray, but cannot help being amused at the acolyte's jeans and tennis shoes under the robe. Then you become embarrassed when you get up and start walking back the wrong way. You feel slightly guilty that you have not felt "holier" during Communion.

That is what the sacraments are: the most sublime moments of the Christian life, but also the most human. There God comes to us—the overwhelming majestic creator of all the galaxies—right where we are most human and worried about so many other mundane and human things. He stoops way down and comes to us in water, bread, and wine, even as we stand there trying rather unsuccessfully to do it just right!

That little splash of water on a crying or a sleeping baby's head, the bit of bread which might stick to the top of your mouth, and that taste of wine—it is at those moments that the background music of the heavens soars to its loudest crescendos, because there God's grace flows most fully to us!

12

From Grace to Grace

Most people define Christianity as a set of beliefs. The first Christians, however, thought of themselves as "followers of Jesus." In the early church they did not think of themselves as a new religion, but as those who belonged to "the Way" (Acts 9:2).

The Gospels make it clear that Jesus came to give us a new way of life. He provided no constitution for a new church. He never outlined a liturgy for his people. He wrote no textbooks or catechisms. In telling us what to do, the one thing he repeated more than anything else was simply: "Love one another."

Of course there are beliefs that undergird this way of life. But in Jesus' view these beliefs are meaningless unless translated into living. His severest criticism was against those people who were overly religious and who had let their religion interfere with loving others.

One of the key verses in Jesus' teaching is John 10:10: "I came that they may have life, and have it abundantly." The Christian faith deals with life, and Jesus himself is "the way, the truth, and the life" (John 14:6). The object of Christianity is not first the teaching, but the teacher and his life.

God's grace is made clear and lived in the life of Jesus, and as we take up his banner and become disciples, this love and grace is given to us, to be soaked up in our own hearts and then flow onward to others. The apostle John puts the sequence very nicely as we have seen:

> In this is love, not that we loved God but that he loved us and sent his Son to be the expiation for our sins. Beloved, if God so loved us, we also ought to love one another (1 John 4:10-11).

We are justified through faith, not works. But in the second breath we must also say that good works flow from faith. We distinguish between faith and works, justification and sanctification, believing and living, but they are all wrapped into one bundle in the Christian life. We are saved by God's grace through faith, but this grace received in faith produces a life in which the love and grace we have received from God are reflected in us.

The Christian is not like a chest of drawers, where faith is in this drawer, love in that, and good works in another. A Christian is like a whole piece of cloth, in which the colors and fabrics are woven together into one.

We can talk all we want about grace. We can write learned books about grace. We can be enormously thankful for God's grace. But if our own lives are not themselves part of grace, then the whole process of Christianity screeches to a halt in a dead-end street.

The goal of the Christian faith and life is that we might echo in our lives the grace that has been given us. God loves us; let us love others. God has forgiven us; let us forgive others. God accepts us even though we are unattractive; let us accept those who are unattractive.

"Credibility" is a favorite word these days. It means that we Christians are believable only when we practice what we preach. There is no way the world can determine whether or not Jesus rose from the dead. But the world can see very well whether or not Jesus' followers reflect in their lives the message of the resurrection which they proclaim.

In a technical sense the means of grace are the Word and sacraments. But in the whole framework of Christian mission another means of grace are the lives of those who follow Jesus, showing in their lives the grace they have received from him. The Word carries power within itself, but a congregation gives a more powerful witness not only by proclaiming the Word, but also by living it.

A Christian missionary was preaching to an audience in India. During the sermon a woman walked out, so the missionary assumed she had rejected his message. Later however she returned and listened more intently than before. As he had talked about God's love for others, she had gone out and asked his coachman how the missionary treated the members of his own household. When she heard of his kindness and generosity, only then was she willing to listen to his message. In time she became a Christian.

Can a person really understand grace if he or she has not seen it in action? Grace is a living thing, and it must be a handicap for people to believe the Word about a loving Father in heaven if they have known only abuse and rejection from their own parents.

I remember a Sunday some years ago when I had spoken about God's love, and after the service a young woman came downstairs for the coffee hour. My wife introduced herself, and in the course of the conversation they talked about the theme of the service. The girl asked, "Is it possible to experience and know the love of God if one has never been loved?" It was not an academic or rhetorical question, but a deeply autobiographical one. She had never known her father. Her mother had been rejected by the rest of the family and had died when the girl was a child. None of the relatives took her in, and she went from foster home to foster home—some good, some not so good, but none permanent. Those were lonely years. But there was a spark in her, and she worked hard in school. Talented in science, she finished an advanced degree. But in spite of the success there was still that hollow place in her heart. She had no church background, but something drew her to our congregation. It was there she learned about grace and love, not only because she heard about it during the service, but also because she found it among the loving people during the coffee hours, potluck suppers, and invitations to homes.

How do you answer, "Can you experience the grace of God if you have not known love from somebody else?" What a monumental hurdle, to trust a loving parent in heaven, when your parents on earth may not have wanted you! It is possible by reading the Bible and hearing the Word, since it does plainly say that God loves us. But God did not intend it to work that way. His intention is that his people are ambassadors for him, and that means that his grace spills over into us, then out to others—from grace to grace.

What a terrible tragedy and judgment it is when Christians do not love others, sometimes not even themselves! Frederick Nietzsche, that miserably unhappy German philosopher who became so disillusioned with Christians, once said, "If you want me to believe in your Redeemer, you'll have to look a lot more redeemed!"

A grotesque mockery of Christianity sometimes takes place when persons become less gracious as they become more "religious." A dose of religion makes them prejudiced and bigoted rather than gracious and understanding toward those with whom they disagree. I knew a young woman who became so religious that she concluded that neither her family, nor her church, nor most of her friends were Christian enough. She became arrogant and judgmental around them, just when she had supposedly discovered Jesus. It seemed to me that she was far more Christian before her experience than after. Strangely, she had become more religious and less Christian!

There is no big secret about how grace goes from person to person. We see it happen among people all the time. If we receive grace, we grow in grace. People have a way of becoming what they are treated as. Treat a youngster like a lying, sneaking delinquent, and in the course of years he may well become a lying, sneaking delinquent. But treat a child with love and respect, and she will very likely grow up treating others with love and respect. There is much truth in Dorothy Nolte's comments about children growing up:

If a child lives with criticism, he learns to condemn.
If a child lives with hostility, he learns to fight.
If a child lives with ridicule, he learns to be shy.
If a child lives with shame, he learns to feel guilty.
If a child lives with tolerance, he learns to be patient.
If a child lives with encouragement, he learns confidence.
If a child lives with praise, he learns to appreciate.
If a child lives with fairness, he learns justice.
If a child lives with security, he learns to have faith.
If a child lives with approval, he learns to like himself.
If a child lives with acceptance and friendship, he learns to find love in the world.

And we could add:

If a child lives with grace, he learns to become gracious.

Some time ago I watched this "dynamic of grace" unfold on the stage in a play that was not at all religious, but which illustrated the drama of grace. It was *Man of La Mancha*, the musical version of *Don Quixote*. Don Quixote is a slightly crazy Spaniard who imagines himself to be a knight. With his squire he arrives at a roadside inn, where the coarse Aldonza is both serving girl and trollop. In a splendid but skewed vision Don Quixote sees her as his dream ideal whom he will serve and adore evermore. He refuses to believe she is anything less than the wonderful lady of his dreams, and he calls her Dulcinea. Aldonza is amused, confused, and finally exasperated by his stubborn and lunatic refusal to see what she really is.

"My lady," he addresses her in courtly fashion, and she sneers back at him,

I am not your lady! I am not any kind of a lady!
    I was spawned in a ditch by a mother who left me
    there
    Naked and cold and too hungry to cry....

    And so I became, as befitted my delicate birth
    the most casual bride of the murdering scum of the
    earth!

Yet something about the old man's vision stirs feelings deep in her heart, for she has never been treated with such esteem and courtesy before. Her abrasive exterior hides the shame she feels for what she is, and she wistfully longs to be a fair Dulcinea. He offers her his quest for an impossible dream, and for just a moment she catches a glimpse of what it would be like to be, indeed, Dulcinea.

She begins to repulse the brutish men of the inn. When she is only laughed at and beaten for her new airs, she turns to Don Quixote and bitterly denounces him for seeing more in her than she is:

Still he torments me! How shall I be a lady?
    Look at me, look at me, God! won't you look at me,
    Look at the kitchen slut reeking of sweat!
    Born on a dung heap to die on a dung heap
    A strumpet men use and forget!
    So please torture me now with your "sweet Dulcineas"
    no more,
    I am no one, I'm nothing, I'm only Aldonza the whore!

But the aged knight will not budge from his vision, and Aldonza is baffled. She has never been treated with such tenderness and respect before, and there is something about his vision that she cannot shake off. As the confused but gallant man is dying, she finally comes to him and pleads with him to rise up again and be the Don Quixote who gave her that vision of glory. In the most moving scene, she leans to him with tears in her eyes and urges him to remember how he used to call her "Dulcinea":

> Please .... try to remember .... you looked at me,
> and you called me by another name ....
>   Dulcinea .... Dulcinea ....
>   When you spoke the name an angel seemed to whisper,
>   Dulcinea .... Dulcinea ....
>
>   Dulcinea .... Dulcinea ....
>   Won't you bring me back the bright and shining glory
>   of Dulcinea .... Dulcinea ....

The old man opens his eyes, grasps her hand and whispers, "Perhaps it was not a dream!"

"Thank you, my Lord!" she answers. After Don Quixote dies, his squire addresses her. She turns to him and replies, "My name is Dulcinea." The knight had treated her as a person of unique worth and value, and she had been transformed.

That is grace. Like Don Quixote, it too is a little crazy, because God treats us not as we really are, but as he wants to treat us—as he wants us to be in his eyes!

Grace does not look at a person with only a coldly analytical eye. Then it would see a sinful person who deserves judgment. But grace looks at us with love. Grace looks for the best in a person. It gives us a new name, just as "Everyman" in John Bunyan's *Pilgrim's*

Progress becomes "Christian" in the course of his pilgrimage. And grace carries within itself such power that the person who is surprised by this unexpected acceptance is caught up and transformed by it.

How have you experienced God in your life? As a vague and distant being? As one who has punished you? As a being whom you fear? When you know his grace, then you are restored and uplifted, and his grace begins to flow outward from you.

A story from my own ministry illustrates how grace can transform. It happened in 1962 in Germany when I was studying at Erlangen University near Nürnberg. On Sundays my wife and I traveled to the U.S. Army base in Bamberg to lead the worship. Two of our dearest friends were a master sergeant and his wife. They had no children and mentioned once that adoption proceedings had been interrupted by this overseas assignment. I asked if they would be interested in adopting a German child. They replied that they would not know where to begin.

During the following week I went to the church office in Nürnberg which handled adoptions and was told that there were few newborns, but many children available. The lady took from her file two pictures of Frederick, a seven-year-old boy and suggested I show them to our friends. Frederick's real parents were not married, and his mother felt she could not take care of him anymore. He was being passed from one foster home to another.

The next Sunday after church, when I showed them Frederick's pictures, it was love at first sight. The next day they picked me up, and we went to Nürnberg. By Friday the paper work had been completed, and Frederick moved in, speaking not a word of English, but now the son of two wonderful people whose army German was limited to *"Danke schön"* and *"Macht's nichts"* ("Thanks" and "It's okay"). After church for the next few Sundays we had to answer the week's accumulated questions from both sides.

But the situation was not quite right. Frederick loved his new home, but he was a frightened little mouse. Maybe this would be just another in the series of homes, and when he was naughty a few times—and what little boy is not naughty a few times?—they would send him back. There was a nervous, almost haunted look in his eyes, as if he just knew this dream would disappear. His new daddy and mommy were trying so hard to be nice, but even the best parents become exasperated sometimes. I just knew this awkward honeymoon could not last forever.

It didn't. One Sunday after church I came out and there was Frederick, hanging out the back of the station wagon. He waved me over and said, *"Weisst Du, was mein Vater mit mir gemacht hat?"* ("Can you guess what my dad did to me?")

I said, no, I couldn't.

With a grin all over his face and eyes sparkling he said with pride in his voice, *"Er hat mich angeschlagen!"* ("He spanked me!")

The story came out. The boy had been naughty, as boys inevitably are. His dad spanked him, as dads do, and Frederick's world crumbled. He ran to his room crying, believing that now it was all over. But this time it was different. His dad followed him into the room, with tears in his own eyes, and swept up the boy in those big arms of his and held him tight. And his mother hugged him, this pitiful little lad from whom love had been pulled away so many times. And through their tears they told him in broken German and simple English that no matter what he did, and no matter if he was naughty, and no matter if they spanked him, he was now their little boy, and nothing in all the world could change that. This was his home, they were his mommy and daddy forever, and nothing or nobody could ever take that away.

It was a moment of pure grace! It was all there—love, acceptance, reconciliation, restoration, new life, rebirth, law and gospel.

From that moment on, his life was never the same. He lived in a whole new situation. He had been accepted, even though he had done nothing to deserve it. He would be naughty again, but that would not change anything. Nothing could ever take away his home and parents.

So he threw back his head and laughed in delight when he told me his dad had spanked him. He was living in the wonder of grace!

Yes, of course he was naughty again—and, yes, his parents disciplined him. But there were always the hugs afterwards. My wife and I have never seen him since those years, but we have followed his progress through Christmas letters, and for a long time a picture of him in his U.S. Navy uniform hung on our bulletin board. Maybe someday he will read these pages and learn something of his own childhood.

It is all a wonder, this whole story of grace. There is not much of it in our tit-for-tat, eye-for-eye world, where we hope at best to get what we deserve. But the story of God's grace has broken into our lives, and once touched and held, we are never the same again!